ASTROLOGY
THROUGH A
PSYCHIC'S
EYES

D1020683

Also by Sylvia Browne

ASTROLOGY
THROUGH A
PSYCHIC'S
EYES

SYLVIA BROWNE

HAY HOUSE, INC.
CARLSBAD, CALIFORNIA • NEW YORK CITY
LONDON • SYDNEY • JOHANNESBURG
VANCOUVER • HONG KONG • NEW DELHI

Copyright © 2000 by Sylvia Browne

Published and distributed in the United States by: Hay House, Inc.:
www.hayhouse.com • *Published and distributed in Australia by:* Hay House
Australia Pty. Ltd.: www.hayhouse.com.au • *Published and distributed in the
United Kingdom by:* Hay House UK, Ltd.: www.hayhouse.co.uk • *Published and
distributed in the Republic of South Africa by:* Hay House SA (Pty), Ltd.:
www.hayhouse.co.za • *Distributed in Canada by:* Raincoast: www.raincoast.com •
Published in India by: Hay House Publishers India: www.hayhouse.co.in

Editorial: Larry Beck, Jill Kramer • *Design:* Jenny Richards

Library of Congress Cataloging-in-Publication Data

Browne, Sylvia.
    Astrology through a psychic's eyes / Sylvia Browne.
        p. cm.
    ISBN 1-56170-720-1 (tradepaper)
    1. Zodiac. 2. Astrology. I. Title.

    BF1726.B76 2000
    133.5—dc21   00-039622

                ISBN 13: 978-1-56170-720-1
                ISBN 10: 1-56170-720-1

        10 09 08 07   16 15 14 13
                1st printing, October 2000
                13th printing, August 2007

            Printed in the United States of America

"Astrology is the mental urging of the mind to come in and work through adversity. No urge exceeds the will of self. No one can detract from the soul; they can only add to it, either positively or negatively. But your will must allow it to be done."

— Francine (Sylvia's spirit guide)

"For now, though, have a good time, and laugh with yourself as well as at yourself. I have done so, and, trust me, it is the only way to health, spirituality, and peace of mind."

— Sylvia

Contents

FOREWORD

This book is Sylvia Browne's statement on astrology. It was written in a humorous vein, yet it is a serious work and is intended to educate the reader. Contained within this book are more than 30 years of joy, tears, laughter, and knowledge—as gathered by Sylvia during her many thousands of counseling sessions.

Sylvia has done extensive research for this book and has used the most reliable data sources available: real people. She feels that astrology is a living discipline and must be studied face-to-face with humanity. Only by a close study of individuals, with all their fears, strengths, phobias, loves, and spirituality, will a true picture of astrology emerge. And as a practicing psychic, she is not misled by the facades people wear.

Sylvia has made her life's work a study of

people, which is now available for you to learn from. We may sit back and enjoy the light she shines upon all of us—her loved ones.

~ Editorial Staff

İntroduction:
Sylvia Browne's Psychic Astrology

Your Sun sign (where the sun was positioned at birth) is characteristic of what you are "made of." The Sun sign presents a view of your *inner* self, that which you feel is you, your fundamental outlook on life. While we will not address all of the planetary aspects, such as the Ascendant and Moon signs (which modify the Sun's influence), you will definitely see yourself in the Sun.

If you intend to dig deeper into astrology, you'll want to know that the Ascendant (also called the "rising" sign, which is the sign rising above the horizon at birth) is the major character backbone, your core essence. The Moon sign (the sign the moon is in at birth) is your entire emotional/personality factor. And remember that you are perfecting over adversity, rather than over wonderfulness.

Midheaven (the sign directly above you at birth) rules finances and career. That is a very important spot. A lot of astrologers, especially when working with progressed charts, will want to know what is happening in your Midheaven. Whatever planets fall into your Midheaven will certainly affect your finances and career.

I have said many times that if 40 Virgos stood up, they would all be in different shapes and sizes. It is ridiculous for astrologers to approach somebody (unless that person is a "pure sign") and say, "I know what you are!" This is because most of the time your structure is actually flavored by the Ascendant, not the Sun. For instance, if your Sun is in Leo and the Ascendant is Libra, more likely than not, the Ascendant will dictate your physical structure, which (for Libra) is to be medium in stature, small-boned, light coloring, with dark eyes.

This book is primarily concerned with the fundamental aspects within your Natal chart (the positions at birth). Yet the basic information may also be used for a "progressed" chart, which allows you to have a daily forecast. Unfortunately, people tend to look upon astrology as a directive. In other words, if you forecast that an accident is coming, it need not be more than just hitting your hand; it does *not* have to be a major accident. You should just take the warning into consideration. But do not go to any extreme such as staying all cooped up in a room—that's ridiculous.

For future reference, keep in mind that the Ascendant and Moon signs, especially the Moon, can flavor everything. People usually refer to their Sun sign when they say, "I am a Pisces," or Leo, or whatever. But the Sun sign alone does not describe the whole character and personality structure.

※ ※ ※

I promise that you will not read any of this information in any other astrology book. This work represents my personal observations from 30 years as a professional psychic. Reading for several thousand people every year has made me somewhat of a statistician. I do *not* ask for a client's sign during a reading, as it does not contribute anything to my work. Rather, after a reading I will ask for their sign to add more data to my collection. After all these years, one really gets a feel for what is going on with the different signs.

You will find that many psychic people have the sign of Libra, Leo, Pisces, Sagittarius, or Aquarius. Now, for God's sake, if your Sun sign is not one of these, do not be upset. You may have the Moon (which is very primary) or the Ascendant in that sign. Therefore, if you are a Virgo or whatever, it does not mean that you cannot be psychic. But it seems like those signs really carry a great deal of psychic impetus in them. So it would stand to reason that a guru would be an earth sign—Virgo, Capricorn, or Taurus—because they are analytical in almost a metaphysical way.

If a person is born on the cusp (the day in which a sign changes), I do not think that they carry traits from both signs. I have seen people born on the cusp who are totally one sign or the other, with little carryover.

Males carry characteristics much more

strongly than the female. The male will take on the full-blown aspects of the sign. This is a general rule of the signs. For example, a Cancer female is never as emotional as her Cancer male counterpart. He is far more martyred and emotional. In other words, he seems to take more depth in a sign for some reason. Now, you would think that the female would be more extreme because of their emotional structure, yet they are not. The same is true for Scorpios. The Scorpio male is much more sexually oriented than the Scorpio female.

So the male takes on the full-blown aspect of a sign. The female of a sign usually takes on more muted qualities. Even in the fire signs, you do not find that the females are nearly as ambitious as the males.

Francine (my spirit guide) says that we go through different signs to take up the task of getting a balance. If we wanted to be more balanced, we would be a Libra; if we wanted to be more ambitious, we would be a Leo; if we wanted to be more practical, we would be a Virgo; and so on and so forth. We take on these aspects when we plan our life prior to incarnating. (I have several other books available that deal with reincarnation and the Other Side, and they're listed at the beginning of this book.)

Francine says that everything is charted for us. We preselect every aspect of our life before incarnating, including our Sun sign, Ascendant, Moon sign, and so on. It is amazing to see the number of children who are born a month "early," or a month "late." They are actually timing their entry to be sure of the right astrological signs. And they are still healthy births. So when you hear of premature children, do not be too upset about it. Most of the time it is just because they did not want one sign—they wanted another one.

Most of the time, you will find that fire and air go very well together. So any of the air signs will go with fire signs, because air feeds fire. Most of the air signs are very fortunate, because they can go with earth and fire and water. But if you get an earth sign with a water sign, then you get murky water, where one muddies up the other one. You really will. Or if you get a very, very strong earth sign and a fire sign, the earth will dampen the fire.

So when you stop and think about it, no one sign goes well with any other sign!

My grandmother (Ada Coil) was a tremendous astrologer. She used to say that three signs away from your own, on both sides (the trine) is very good.

And then there are the "sister signs" (six signs away). Libra and Aries are sister or "twin" signs. They take on twin aspects. Even though one is air and the other is fire, they complement each other.

Years ago, when they really used astrology (such as in Napoleon's time), people would actually pick who would be their general, or who would ride with whom, because of the dynamics of their astrological sign. And most world leaders, such as Caesar, ruled the world by what their astrologers counseled.

Francine says that everyone comes into a sign that is compatible with their theme in life. And as a result, cusp people will possibly be "middle-of-the-road" types. In other words, they really want to perfect a lot. I am convinced that cusp people have a very heavy perfection scheme because they may be pulling from many areas. They are not only picking out Sun signs, but they are pulling from Ascendants, Moon, and so on. We are really talking about a duality—in the truest sense of the word.

Francine also says that, beyond a shadow of a doubt, we do not come in with every single sign in our chart (in one lifetime). If you wanted to correct moodiness, you would come in with water signs to overcome that (because they tend to have moods). Or perhaps you do not want to be so flighty, so you would come in as an air sign to perfect over that (because air signs tend to be impractical). For example, when signs are married, there can be a problem if one is down, the other is down, or when one is up, the other is up. They can reflect one another.

A rule of thumb is that you are compatible with someone who is three signs removed from you, in either direction. But they are not the only people you get along with. Francine says that during our evolution, we pull certain signs to us that are either compatible or irritating—

again, to aid in one's perfection of the soul.

People born in the fall and winter "blossom" later in their life, where spring and summer people will blossom earlier in their life. Now that does not mean that they go to pot afterwards, but they will pursue their profession and goals early in life, where the other ones will change later on.

Fall, and especially winter, babies, are supposed to be much smarter than any of the other signs. No one knows why, but statistics show this to be true.

Parallels

All parallel signs seem to be alike, in a complementary manner. It is the sister part of you. This is the duality, or balance, of you. For example, Gemini is very airy and somewhat flighty, whereas Sagittarius (the parallel to Gemini) is quite analytical. So we see a direct balance within the parallels, which are:

♈ Aries and Libra ♎
♉ Taurus and Scorpio ♏

♊ Gemini and Sagittarius ♐
♋ Cancer and Capricorn ♑
♌ Leo and Aquarius ♒
♍ Virgo and Pisces ♓

Can you see how this works? You will notice from the list that one sign is very analytical, and one is more flighty, but it is a good balance overall.

Now, I am not like most astrologers who say, "For God's sake, if you do not marry a certain sign, you will never be happy." This is because we have to get into the Ascendant and into some planetary positions (Venus and Mercury) to fully determine marriage partners.

The next chapters describe in detail each Sun sign of the zodiac. This information is the result of my counseling work with thousands of people. It represents a 30-year summary of my observations, psychic insights, and the personal histories of my clients. Please enjoy what follows, and laugh along with me. . . .

Sun Sign Information

Natal Signs/Ruling Planets

♈ **Aries:** March 21–April 19 / *Mars*

♉ **Taurus:** April 20–May 20 / *Venus*

♊ **Gemini:** May 21–June 20 / *Mercury*

♋ **Cancer:** June 21–July 22 / *Moon*

♌ **Leo:** July 23–August 22 / *Sun*

♍ **Virgo:** August 23–September 22 / *Mercury*

♎ **Libra:** September 23–October 22 / *Venus*

♏ **Scorpio:** October 23–November 21 / *Pluto*

♐ **Sagittarius:** November 22–December 21 / *Jupiter*

♑ **Capricorn:** December 22–January 19 / *Saturn*

♒ **Aquarius:** January 20–February 18 / *Uranus*

♓ **Pisces:** February 19–March 20 / *Neptune*

Characteristics of the Signs

Air: *Mental*	Libra	Gemini	Aquarius
Water: *Emotional*	Cancer	Pisces	Scorpio
Earth: *Practical*	Capricorn	Virgo	Taurus
Fire: *Ambitious*	Aries	Sagittarius	Leo
	Cardinal	*Mutable*	*Fixed*
	Active	Passive	Stable
	Enterprising	Adaptable	Resistant to change

Physical Traits

Aries: Short to medium height; medium-boned; tendency to get heavy; square jawline

Taurus: Short; heavy-boned; short neck, magnetic eyes; stumbles a lot; tendency to put on weight and cannot take it off

Gemini: Real short to medium height; light-boned; flighty movements; unimposing in speech; heavy head of hair

Cancer: Tall; large bones; full-bodied; round face; cherubic looking; limpid eyes; hesitant in speech

Leo: Tall; graceful body; feet point outward; heavy hair; distinctive walk; rigid backbone

Virgo: Tall to very tall; heavy movements; large features; round eyes; fair complexion; walks with a slanted hitch; moves with purpose; peers out of the corners of their eyes a lot

Physical Traits, cont'd.

Libra: Medium to tall; delicate bones; never still; always in motion; prides themselves on feet and hands; light coloring; dark eyes; adorned

Scorpio: Tall; can gain weight easily even as a child; deep, impenetrable eyes, slanted or squinty; graceful walk and mannerisms; opaque gestures

Capricorn: Tall to very tall; angular bone structure; hooded eyes, usually slanted upward; brown to reddish hair; lopsided grin; pale complexion

Sagittarius: Round-faced; medium build; small eyes; sharp features; quick movements; meticulous regarding their dress

Aquarius: Medium to short in height; small-boned; delicate facial structure; lots of dark hair; puppy dog eyes; full lips

Pisces: Very tall; beautiful feet; they dance when they walk; beautiful round, large eyes; sweet and vulnerable face; childlike expressions at any age

Emotional Traits

Aries: Proud, aggressive, set in their ways

Taurus: Stubborn, loyal, with a single focus

Gemini: Multifaceted, does two things well, fanatical

Cancer: Martyred, home-loving, security conscious

Leo: Proud, loyal, loves children, fickle

Virgo: Can love two at once, unbending

Libra: Justice minded, wordy, lover of beauty

Scorpio: Intense, secretive, hurts easily

Sagittarius: Tend to be doctors, analytical, fastidious

Capricorn: Strong, nitpicky

Aquarius: Fluid-moving, changeable

Pisces: Very sensitive, overly generous, obsessive

The Sun Signs

Aries

Aries is the sign characterized by people with impulsive and compulsive personalities. They are very avid learners—but they will only learn what they *want* to learn. The other fire signs, Leo and Sagittarius, will learn things that they don't necessarily want to simply because they feel they *need* to know these things. An Aries is not the type of person to take a generalized humanities course, but will be riveted into specialization, usually becoming an authority on some subject.

Arians will only get into subjects that are totally involved with themselves—things that will aid and help them, so to speak. That is why they will study astrology—it tells them about themselves. Like the other fire signs, Arians are also very loyal. Most of the Arians that I have known and dealt with over the years are very fanatical about certain things. If Arians get religion—God help you—because they are going to give it to you! They are not what I would call crazy fanatics, but boy—they get on one binge, and it's a lifelong one. So they don't change horses in midstream. They will put their allegiance someplace, and that's it—it will not waver.

Don't tell Arians that their beliefs are wrong, because Aries is the one sign that will just deck you. They don't mess around with you. But at the same time, to get rid of an Aries is almost impossible. If you have ever been married to an Aries individual, or have any dealings with one, and you get fed up with them for any reason, you cannot shake this person! It is almost impossible; Arians will dog your heels.

Arians have a beautiful, almost charming way of leading with their chin. They step in where angels fear to tread, and they almost beg you to go along with them. When no one else will taste a certain food, it is the Aries who says, "Oh, to hell with it! I'll try it!" Or if someone says not to walk somewhere, the Aries will say, "Forget it! I'm going over there."

Arians are the ones who will typically step into any kind of joke. If you want to make a joke work, run to an Aries and say, "Knock, knock . . ." because this person will immediately take the bait—every time! Arians are so inquisitive that they must say, "Who's there?"—even if they don't want to. And if you ever want a straight man, put an Aries beside you. These individuals have the naïveté to give you the most beautiful openings for jokes.

A very beautiful thing about Arians is that they not only laugh *with* you, but they can also laugh at themselves. Not many signs can do that very well. If Arians find themselves in compromising situations, they will laugh right along, even when they are totally off-kilter. And Arians have the ability to make a joke out of their own embarrassment, so everybody laughs with them. They have that natural charm.

Arians are very good writers of documents, especially legal ones. Even though much of their writing can be boring and scientific, it is quite factual. Arians will prove a point to the "nth degree," when speaking or writing. They will go over and over something because they're convinced that you're too dumb to get it the first time. They ought to all teach kindergarten, because then they could go over and over and over information again with those little, itty-bitty people. They feel compelled to repeat something four times, in four different ways. You will finally say, "Okay, I give up, I believe you, anything you want!" What is amazing, though, is that once you prove your intelligence to an Aries, he or she will usually back down, but not until you have proven your worth beyond any shadow of a doubt. After proving your intelligence to Arians, they do not tend to "hog the show." They will let you have equal time, which is an amazing thing about them. But, my God, the effort needed to prove it!

An Aries can work marvelously with any group of people, even the senile or the handicapped. This is not to demean such people, but the Aries could go over things 140 times with no problem. They would know that they have a captive audience there, and they have all the patience in the world. You never want to turn your back on Arians when they're talking to you, though. That is the most horrible affront, because they know that what they say is important for you to hear. And if you turn your back on them, that is an unforgivable sin.

Arians do not like change. They want to know that the same building has stood for 50 years. If something is torn down, they don't like it at all. They will say, "Remember that place on Bascom Avenue that stood there? And now look what they did to it!"

Arians are also tremendously involved with their own childhood, where many signs are not. They will tell you what they did at age four, three, two, and one . . . and have slides and movies to go with it. They will tell you what they did when they were a kid. And you say, "Who cares?" Arians will also evaluate things by how they were done when they were children: "When I was a child, it was done this way."

What is really amazing about Arians is that they have really refined the art of sarcasm. And you cannot help but love these individuals because even with their sarcasm, they are funny! After an Aries gets through with you, you stand bleeding and laughing at the same time, because it's so funny. And Arians don't feel that they have been that sarcastic at all. They will say, "I merely stated it as it is."

Arians are very loyal and protective of their family unit—or of anybody they have absorbed into their family unit. They are tremendously loyal and adoptive people. They will take a person, and they will say, "You are just like my mother, or like my sister." So you will be absorbed immediately into their family unit— whether you like it or not! You are the second mother, or second sister, or whoever! If you are ever in a battle about anything, you want an Aries on your side. There is no doubt about that. But you had better make darn certain that they *are* on your side. You do not want to go into battle where the Aries has a predisposition for the other person, because then you could get annihilated. Leos think they have big mouths, but Arians far surpass them. I would never want to go up against a Leo and an Aries, especially together.

The Aries will usually be found in technical work, law, documentary writing, graphics, or anything that has to do with forms, statistics, managing, and overseeing. And they are inventors—they could be called the inventors of the zodiac. They will have ideas and pull in thoughts that no one has ever dreamed of. And they can make them work. "This wire goes in here; and I know I can make this." And they simply do it.

In their early years, Arians are tremendous gatherers of information and concepts. Then in midyears and later life, they will draw on this wealth of knowledge. They also have a marvelous retentive memory (although not the "file cabinet" mind of Libras), but they just retain an amazing amount of trivia. They know exactly how many light-years away such-and-such is, and so forth.

Arian attention to trivia is similar to the Capricorn trait of detail retention. Yet Arians get very aggravated with Capricorns, because

Arians do not care to know if it was Tuesday or Wednesday when they wore the blue suit. The Aries could not care less, while the Capricorn is concerned with such details. No fire sign wants to put up with that. Libras and the other air signs will sit there yawning away, and the fire sign will say, "Get to the point!" They just come right out and say it. And the water sign just floats away with it—they couldn't care less. The water sign will say, "I am going to go into my own alpha state, and I don't care."

Arians need their own space—but it is usually their own constructed space, which is different from other people. In other words, they get very territorial: "This is my niche, my stereo, my desk, and my eraser." But they don't have to go out into the wilderness like some of the other signs do. Some signs will say, "Give me wide open spaces, give me the desert, give me the ocean, give me . . ." But an Aries would rather have their time alone in their own workroom. They just need a little place that is theirs to hang up their shingle. And they have to do all their own little charts and their own little diagrams and their other little things. They will

spend many hours alone, and they need their
secluded time. If they had an air sign hovering
over them saying, "Notice me, notice me . . .,"
it would drive them crazy.

It is best to let Arians work independently;
they do not work well with somebody domi-
nating them all of the time. Just tell an Aries
what to do, and then let them do it. You cannot stand over Arians and dictate to them; you
would make them crazy. No fire sign likes to
be dominated, but especially the Aries. They
do not want to be pushed around. Usually
Arians are thinking way ahead of the boss anyway, and they will always want to tell their
supervisor how to do it better. This does not go
over too well with that person, as you can
imagine. Leos, on the other hand, will say,
"That's your problem!" and walk away because
they get fed up and that's the end of it.

If you can finally establish a working relationship with an Aries, and convince this person that *you* are the boss, then he or she will
respect you and not force everything to be
their way. But it takes several years to reach
that understanding. I spent five years saying,

"I'm the boss!" every morning to my Aries employee.

Most Arians have very loud speaking voices, and I do not mean projection. You get the feeling that you are deaf when you're around Arians—or you soon will be—because when you're sitting right next to them, they will yell at you! Even when they're "whispering," they will blast out, "Did you see that?" You then tell them, "Shhh, that's not a whisper—it's more like a stage whisper," and they say, "I *am* speaking quietly!" They even yell on the phone. Most of the water signs are more soft-spoken. The air and the fire signs seem to have the louder voices.

Physical Characteristics

♈   Arians have naturally agile bodies. They can be very good dancers; and they are very fluid when moving. If you have ever watched Arians walk, they tend to undulate in some way.

♈   Arians have a lot of problems with their teeth, but they do not want to take care of them.

♈   Anyone fiddling around with the mouth or face of an Aries drives them crazy. Usually you will not find them with tight collars on, either. They do not like anything around their neck—especially if your hands happen to be around their throat, choking them!

♈   Their feet give them a lot of problems; most of the time they are born with flat feet.

♈   And like some of the other signs, the spinal area gives Arians problems, as well as the lower intestinal tract.

♈   Arians are usually light-complected, even if they have dark hair. Their whole visage seems to be light in color.

TAURUS

Have you read any other astrology books? Well, if so, then you know beyond a shadow of a doubt that there is always one sign that the astrologer does not like. That's because when you read about the various signs, both the positive and negative aspects are discussed. But then you get to one particular sign, and you realize that there seems to be nothing but negative traits associated with it. Well, I'm going to have to be very tolerant with the sign of Taurus, and I've got to be kind about this . . . *God*, I have to be kind!

Taurus people are boring. I'm trying to be

kind, but every Taurus that I have ever known (and I mean a fully aspected Taurus[1]) has a tendency toward stupidity. Yet I do not think that they *are* actually that dumb, but they act that way. They will often reply to questions with "Huh?" and a puzzled look. I think this is to make someone come on more. You will want to walk up and say, "Do you hear me? Are you listening? Watch my lips!"

Everyone who has a Taurus friend has a karmic debt! Even when you say, "Get away," they hang on to your leg. You can beat them with a stick, and they say, "I love you anyway." An Aries ought to work with a Taurus, for God's sake, because they've got enough patience. The Aries would repeat things 55 times, and the Taurus would say, "I finally get it," which would make the Aries say, "Oh, how wonderful!"

Taureans usually have very high-falutin' speech. They usually talk like this: "The cosmic influences of the seminal fluid, in the great beyond of the ad infinitum, are coming together

---

[1] By "fully aspected," I mean that no other aspects (planetary alignments) negate the Taurus traits.

in the heated vortex within." You then say, "Pardon me, but I do not understand a thing you're saying." In this instance, they just asked you to have sex, without your even knowing it!

Taureans are also very poetic in their speech, which seems contrary to their sign. But they always sound like they're going to break into Shakespeare, which seems like a paradox because they're so thick. They can think of 16 different ways to say something beautifully. And this is the sign that gets drunk on words. Their verbalization pattern is something to behold.

Taurus is the sign of the bull, and bulls are definitely stubborn. This is basically how you can spot a Taurus: Hell hath no fury like Taureans on a rampage; they will walk over anybody. But it is usually out of righteous anger, because they are ruled by Venus, the love planet. So this is not a malicious sign. Yet, don't get Taureans mad at you, because they're vindictive and will absolutely stalk you—like an elephant.

Taureans do not forget past injustices, and they also remember their past pain as well—

and will remind you of it. The tragedy with a Taurus is that their pain is just as fresh today as it was the first time. Their pain will often make you feel guilty, and if you tell them about your guilt, they will tell you to think nothing of it. So they're not malicious; but they do become very martyred.

It has always been said that the water signs are martyred, but Taureans outdo them all. Taureans can be the biggest martyrs in the world. They will tell you what they've done for you, when they did it, why they did it, and how they did it. They tend to live in the past a lot. If you're married to a Taurus, this individual will tell you about their past romances, and they will go into details about the whole situation. They want to tell you and confess all, which is called "spilling your guts." Not only that, they will tell you how much better you are than their previous lovers—but that still doesn't stop them from telling you too many details.

Taurus is an earth sign. Some astrologers say that earth signs are base. Taureans are not base or crude, though. Taureans, of all the earth signs, are really very high-flown and poetic. Many times they will go on for years in a very beautiful, platonic relationship. So their primary motive is not just to bed you down. Not at all. They can simply love people for the love that they have for them. I would not call them a tremendously sensual sign at all. They put out sensuality—but they are not necessarily that sensual. It is much like talking a good story, but the action is lacking.

If you end a relationship with a Taurus, this person will stalk you for years and years after. Taureans are obsessive about wanting to know what caused the breakup. They are much like Arians in that way. And what is really amazing about Taureans—and I have never seen this to fail—is that they are not really affectionate as far as touching, but they do have a tendency to tweak you. They will tweak and punch and pinch—they will walk up to both cheeks and pinch them.

Taureans are very aesthetic in all forms— writing, acting, music, and so on. You will find a lot of actors and actresses under the sign of Taurus. And they do have a natural flair for design, colors, and that type of thing. All earth signs have this. They are also marvelous sales people and can sell you anything. You may even have buyer's remorse at the time you purchase something, and yet you find yourself signing on the dotted line. They really are the manipulators of the zodiac, but they do it in such an ingenious way that you don't mind, at least not with a true Taurus. Taureans can be so glib, smoothing over everything, that you're doing what they want before you realize it. You may say, "I don't want to do this, but here I am doing it!"

Taureans are the type of individuals who will take your advice, saying, "Thank you very much," then go and do things exactly the way they were doing it before—but they will thank you for the advice. If you had told them about a new shortcut that would save them time, they would say thank you and use the old, long way instead. A Taurus can be led, but never pushed.

Taureans are really "in service" individuals—that is, they will always let you know that they have performed some service for you. The only tragedy here is that they will constantly remind you of it. Even in their sexual life, they say, "Are you pleased that I . . . . Are you thankful for it?" So they need to be in your service—sexually or otherwise—and you should be grateful.

Taureans have a habit of asking how you like everything—a movie, dinner, tea, or whatever. "Did you like that?" they will ask repeatedly. They also have a habit of watching you to see if you're enjoying something, such as a play or movie. If you're listening to a record, they watch to see if you're enjoying it—which, of course, makes you an animated goof after a while.

Ecology and all growing things are of great concern to Taureans. This is because they are very concerned about the earth, its growth, and what will be left here for future generations. They are horticulturists, and they always have something growing someplace.

Neatness is very important to Taureans, too. In fact, they can drive you crazy with their finickiness. If by chance they are not neat, then even within the chaos, there is organization. No matter what the mess, they know where everything is. You ask, "Where is that paper?"

and they say, "In the other room on the desk." And you're afraid to enter that room because you know a rat will jump out and get you. So you walk into the room and yell back, "You've got to be kidding. I can't find anything in here!" The Taurus will then come in and say, "There it is. Two sheets down, over to the right, under the dirty hanky, and I found it!" So this individual knows exactly where it is. Therefore, there must be some kind of a filing system going on there. They know where all the trivia is in their mind, as well as all the trivia in the house.

The Taurus is not as nitpicky as the Capricorn, though. When Capricorns do something, they will tell you the exact day of the week, what clothes they wore, how they did it, the weather, and if it was 2:12 or 2:13 P.M. when it happened. And you say, "Oh, yuck!" Taureans are mental note takers, and they also make lists for themselves every day, usually posting them. Not only that, but if you allow them to, they will make lists for *you*, too. They have to make sure that everything will be all right.

Taureans will fall madly in love, and they are a very flirtatious sign. They are not like Virgos, or some of the other signs, who can be in love with three people, equally and all at once. But Taureans can love many—they are very magnanimous, and they can love people collectively. "I love all of you," they say, and they are not kidding about it. They really love everyone.

Taureans are really not lovers of home and family, although they will *keep* a home and have a family. I would not call them the primary motherhood or fatherhood signs. They're just not. They will procreate and leave it at that—it is there, it is all right, and they will give allegiance. But there is no ego structure involved with the act of creation. They do not say, "This is what I made, this child before you." To a Taurus, you will say, "Oh, your little boy is so cute," and they will reply, "He's all right, fine, he will do." Most of the other signs feel that this is a reflection on themselves. But Taureans say, "Well, I did it, everyone does, big deal." They still show great allegiance to their children, but they are simply not overwhelmed with the fact of having them. It is a natural thing to do.

Taureans do not care much for genetics, heritage, family roots, and the like. They view people as singularly unique, rather than a collection of traits from their ancestors. They tend to say, "I exist, which is enough for me, and so do you, and that is all there is."

A Taurus can get totally furious instantaneously, for no apparent reason. You will back up, saying, "What started that, anyway?" What you do not want to see is a Taurus go at it with a fire sign. It is unbelievably violent. The fire sign is determined to keep the earth sign from putting a damper on them. When a Taurus is arguing with you, it feels as though your whole identity is in jeopardy. They can really slash you, out of pain or vulnerability, but the cutting can go very deep.

Taureans are the champions at being possessive, beyond anything you can imagine. Yet they do not strangle you with it. It is more a concern about your health, welfare, and safety. "Where were you? You didn't call me, and I was worried. You said you would be home at

8:00, and it is now 8:02 P.M. What happened?" So don't leave a Taurus hanging, walking the floor; they worry too much.

I do not know where all of the Taureans are. I ask people, "Do you know any Taureans?" They always say no. Nobody seems to know any of them. I think they crawled under a rock, and that is the end of them.

Taureans are usually very sentimental. They never forget birthdays, anniversaries, and so forth. First thing in the morning, they'll say, "Do you know what day it is?" Strike up the band—it's someone's birthday!

Taureans tend to be very affluent. They make money, and they mark their success by how much money they can generate. Every Taurus male that I know of has become a lawyer and bought property. Even the females will buy property. They are homesteaders. They don't care if it's a shack; they put their sign on it: "I own this."

Taureans have total tunnel vision. If they become fixed on one thing, hell hath no fury like a Taurus, because they go forging right ahead in the face of all obstacles. And they do not see danger on either side; they simply have a goal and go right for it.

Physical Characteristics

♉ Even though Libra is air and Taurus is earth, they are both ruled by Venus. So you will find that many Taureans are very light-eyed, have light hair, and are finely boned (a true Taurus, anyway). However, they do have thick necks.

♉ Taurus is marked by beautiful, expressive hands. The males' hands look like surgeons' hands, and the females look like they should model their hands in commercials.

♉ Taureans are very nicely built; everything is compact and seems to fit right into place. They always seems to be evenly proportioned, even if they're heavy. I don't know whether they dress like that, but they always look okay.

You are always deceived by Taureans' weight, too, because they look slimmer than they really are.

♉ Weak eyes and weak hearing are a problem for Taureans. Maybe that's why they scream so much.

♉ The Taurus nervous system is very ticklish. "That's enough!" they will shout when annoyed. So you don't want to grate on their nerves very long.

♉ Taureans are very sensitive to smells and sounds, because they are sensory-oriented people. Their sensory input is brilliant; they like beautiful colors and sounds.

Gemini

Gemini is an air sign, and Geminis are known for being avid talkers. With Geminis, you want to say, "But . . . but . . . ," but you never get a chance. They will talk to you for two hours on the phone, and all you've said is three "buts." Like some of my clients, you will say, "Gee, it's been nice talking to you." But in truth, they did all of the talking, and you didn't tell them anything. However, usually this is not until the Gemini gets rolling.

Geminis are very reticent until they're certain that they have you in their pocket, so to speak. They are careful about giving you their allegiance, and they are probably the most cautious sign of the zodiac.

Geminis use their hands even more than Libras, or any other sign. They are very expressive and are always motioning with their hands and feet. They cannot talk without using them, and I'm talking about highly exaggerated gestures. They also have a tendency to watch themselves a lot. They're always concerned about their pose—and their poise. You will find Geminis looking at themselves to see if everything is right—if the hand on the leg looks right. They have a tendency to check themselves because they're insecure. You will never find Geminis making a crazy face or sitting in a slouchy manner. They want to look good at all times.

Geminis are also very concerned about learning. If you see a Gemini who does not have a full education, they will tell you about it until their last day on Earth. You wish to God you could give them the money so they could go to school and finish it off. Get them as high as they can go—a Ph.D. or whatever—so they will quit telling you that if "I only had the chance, I would have gone further." They always feel a bit deficient if they do not have extensive schooling.

Every teacher needs Geminis in class, because even though they seem to miss the information, they do absorb everything. They are the only sign I know of that takes 50 years to get something done. Most of your "professional students" are Geminis. They are always working on some lofty degree over there somewhere. And I don't think they will ever get there. But they are constantly working toward it.

There is a lot of movement with Geminis. They are always moving toward some far-off, unreachable dream. They will get channeled into one thing, then the first thing you know, they are into something else.

The ancient symbol of two faces is used for Gemini. Now, I do not believe what most astrologers say—that the left hand does not know what the right hand is doing, or that they are split personalities. I do *not* believe that. What Geminis do have, though, are very changeable natures, so you don't know what face they are going to wear. And they can do so many things at once—they can have two or three things going all at the same time. I think they're so multifaceted that you ask, "Who are you today?" They seem to be able to take on different faces and aspects daily.

Others cannot keep up with Geminis; you will feel like you're on a pogo stick. They are highly mutable and versatile. They become highly aggravated if you can't keep up with them. You'll say, "But we were just on one train of thought, and now you're way over here." And they say, "But I finished that, and now I'm here." They really question your intelligence when you can't keep up with them. However, Geminis know so much about so many things because they've had a whole lifetime of jumping around.

Geminis have the amazing ability to hear what they want to hear, which all signs have, to some extent. But if you say something to Geminis, they will "repeat" it back to you and you'll wonder where the heck it came from. You think it is an entirely different concept. They do not hear what has just been said. They seem to absorb at the subconscious level for some reason, through the process of osmosis.

Geminis really are the "infused knowledge" sign. They are also the echo sign. You will get all finished saying something, and they will repeat the same concept back, and you'll say, "That's just what I said!" They reply, "Well, not *exactly*. You did not fill it in right, you see. Now, *I* have said it correctly."

Geminis can change loves, careers, and geographical locations, and be perfectly happy with all of it. They are the wanderers of the world. They will change whole cultures and whole structures because they're so fluid. Not many signs can move geographically as fast as the Gemini. You will find that Geminis infrequently stay in the same location where they grew up.

Geminis become fascinated with races, cultures, and sociological structures. They will even go to a reservation and live for a while to see how it is. If they can't go, they fantasize about it. They'll say, "Gee, it would be marvelous to live like that." Or, a Gemini will become a hippie for a while to see how it is, and then change into something else again dramatically. They are the experimenters of the zodiac.

You wonder sometimes how much depth there is to Geminis, because they do seem to live on the surface of the world. However, they do have great depth. And if there is any sign that walks around saying that "life is a bowl of cherries," it is the Gemini. This can really help cheer everyone up. Geminis can be totally immersed in grief and sorrow, yet 15 minutes later, they'll say, "Let's have a party!" You may still be wallowing in the grief with them, and here they are blowing up balloons!

Most of the Geminis I've known, male and female, do not sustain long-lasting relationships. They can have a totally ingrained family structure, and the first thing you know, they're divorced, off on a boat with someone new, married again, and are perfectly happy with two more kids. They're very fickle, and they'll love you just as much as they can, but you're really talking about a thimbleful versus a cupful. I think this is because they scatter their love so much. They will love their children and their parents and their teacher and whomever. So they're scattering love throughout all of the rest of the zodiac.

Geminis are fun, and you want to have them around you. They are the exuberant sign of the zodiac, and nothing bothers them. They could be 58 years old and say, "Let's go to the amusement park." Or they could be in a wheelchair, and the Gemini is the first one up the roller coaster—wheels and all. Everyone should have a Gemini as a pet, because they make good ones. The Gemini friends in school are the ones you could call up and say, "Oh, let's go out and buzz the drive-ins, let's do this, let's do that . . ." They are always ready to go.

Marriages with Geminis will only do well if their spouse totally understands that they must flit from flower to flower. And I don't mean that they'll flit among romances. But they *will* say, "I am involved here with underwater basket weaving." And then, "Now I want to take a psychology course." The mate does not understand what they're doing! The Gemini can become very enamored with something, with parapsychology or anything else, and then the first thing you know, they're tired of it and involved with something else.

So Geminis do not stay grounded. Usually with a Gemini, you will see a long-suffering spouse standing there. You must have *one* stable spouse. Actually, I'm convinced that the best sign with a Gemini is fire, because they're very stable, and they do burn bright. The fire sign can sustain this bouncing type of thing, because the fire sign gives them stability. And fire signs are normally not too restrictive because they like a lot of space themselves. The air signs should really link up with fire signs, because they can totally channel their energies independently.

The Gemini can just flit around and do their own thing, and the fire sign says, "Well, whenever you're ready, come home, because I'm doing my own thing anyway." Of course this depends on how you start out and what you're accustomed to. It depends a lot on your conditioning. But you will find that air and fire signs make a marvelous combination, really, because air fans fire. And they can sustain each other very, very well.

Geminis can become very affected in

speech; they are very didactic. However, they are not like Taureans, with their high-flown speech. But all of a sudden, Geminis can start talking with a southern accent. And they say, "Where did that come from?!" Or they will affect a lisp, or baby talk. You never want to tell Geminis that you think they're illiterate, because whatever they don't know, they will fake. You don't want to say to them, "My God, have you never heard of Rhett and Scarlett?" The Gemini will say, "Oh, certainly I have—they were two dogs, weren't they?" And you feel so sorry for them that you say, "Yes, yes, they were," because you don't want to put them down, which would annihilate them.

Physical Characteristics

♊ Geminis are short and dainty in their physical structure.

♊ They are usually dark—dark-haired, dark-eyed. Their eyes are very promi-nent. They can either be slanted or they have full lids, so they always have what is called "bedroom eyes"—a slow "come hither" look.

♊ Like Leos, most Geminis have beautiful manes of silky-fine, glossy hair.

♊ And, as mentioned earlier, they have highly expressive hands and feet.

CANCER

JUNE 21–JULY 22

Cancer is a water sign—a maudlin, martyred sign. Cancer is really the sign that carries a cross around, and sure enough, people will hoist them up on it.

Cancers are home-loving, protective individuals. They are very attached to their children. The males make good fathers, and the females consider motherhood their job. It is their whole life, and they will tell you that. When they say to their children, "I have given up my whole life for you," it's true!

Cancers find parting with money very difficult. They will be unbelievably frugal in some areas, and absolutely frivolous in others. They also tend to be immaculate in their grooming, but quite messy in their surroundings.

Cancers view life almost too mystically and romantically. No matter how old they get, they really *love* love. They love the romance and wine of life. They must guard against alcohol and drugs, as they can fall into excesses very easily. They are also painfully shy and often-times demure in affairs of the heart. It does not come easily for them to speak eloquently, but they can write very well. In fact, all water signs are good at letting their pen speak.

Cancers adore animals, and while they lean toward cats and large animals, their love encompasses all living things. They have green thumbs, so they're good with plants, gardens, and farming. The simple life is best for Cancers. Too much stress puts a strain on their delicate balance, and their nerves will give out.

Cancers are very selective, probably one of the most particular signs of the zodiac. They do not have a massive number of friends during their life. If they're honest, they will admit to having just one true friend. I think the reason is that all of their love, time, and energy is devoted to their family, which can create a "martyr" situation. In giving so much of themselves, they have no time for personal activities and begin to feel left out.

If Cancers are attached to an organization, they will give endless time and service, far beyond the call of duty, to the group. They make marvelous employees; in fact, you can give them an impressive title and lower their salary!

If you ever tell Cancers that they can't do something, they will immediately say, "Why not?" then go right out and do it. So the one thing *not* to tell a Cancer is, "I do not think you should . . ."

Cancers *do* have moods, but they have been given a very bad reputation in astrology, because although they're prone to moodiness, a Cancer will actually try harder to get *out* of the mood. They fight an innate, depressing type of metabolism, so it's a pathological problem. You'll find them having problems with the thyroid, gall bladder, pancreas, blood sugar, and gland-related areas.

If you hurt a Cancer, you'll think you've committed a cardinal sin. When you hurt them, they do not slap back at you. Instead, they give you a really doe-eyed, "You killed me" look that makes you feel extremely guilty. It's a classic "Sarah Bernhardt" all the way, and you know that you're the villain. You've killed them, it's all over, and you've destroyed their life. You say, "I'm sorry, I'm sorry, I'm sorry." Then when you ask them what is wrong, they say, "Nothing!" Yet four days later, they'll say, "Remember when you said blah, blah, blah—well, it hurt my feelings." And they're still hurt, deeply. In fact, Cancers are hurt so easily that you don't even want to say, "I think your pants would look better if you wore them a little bit longer." They take it to mean that you think they don't dress right, and look tacky. But most Cancers *realize* that they can be hurt easily and can be moody, so they almost work themselves out of it. The nice thing about Cancers is, even though they're hurt and sustain it for days, they forgive you later.

Cancers will categorize—by date, hour, and minute—every hurt ever dealt to them. Even though they'll forgive you, they don't forget about the event.

Cancers have more than an insecurity; it is actually an inferiority that they're born with. They have an obsession with appearing stupid, sometimes so much so that they get harassed and fulfill their own dreaded prophecy of being dumb.

There is always a subliminal depression they operate with, which is due to their glands. When the glands are so "ticklish," God, you have a hard row to hoe.

Cancers have the ability to tell you the same story 85 times. And for some reason, they never reach the punchline. You don't ever want to let a Cancer tell jokes, because the punchline comes out first, and then they'll forget the rest. However, they're not disconcerted by this at all. They know they can't tell jokes, and they'll tell you as much. So you're left sitting there, saying, "But what about the dog . . . ?" Cancers have a good memory, though. How else could they tell the same story over and over again? It's because they have every story categorized!

Cancers have a marvelous laugh. You can

always tell a Cancer by their very hardy, full laugh. They're usually amused by anything that's not in correct order—in other words, not so much by slapstick, but anything that is off-kilter. For example, Cancers will laugh at drunks because they're not following the normal way of doing things.

Cancers have a natural aptitude for knowing when something is not right, and they find it hilariously funny. However, they're not practical jokers; their hypersensitivity keeps them from being that way. They lean more toward the mental side of humor, or anything that is displaced. Humor is almost a catharsis for them; it's a release factor for their sense of inferiority. They view humor as something *else* being displaced, because Cancers walk around most of their lives feeling displaced. I think it's because they're fighting their mood changes.

Every Cancer that I've driven with, regardless of their age, drives like a little old person. At age 20, they're driving like a senile octogenarian. They are very cautious, convinced that somebody's going to pull out from a side street and smack them a good one. So they drive with both hands on the steering wheel, with tense white knuckles. You'll never find a Cancer out on a speedway—not a full Cancer. They're not going to take any chances.

Physical Characteristics

♋ Cancers are very glandular and metabolically oriented; they must watch their diet very closely.

♋ They have problems with circulation. Anything that has to do with the thyroid or the chakras seems to be attacked very severely.

♋ Cancers have problems with their blood sugar and pancreas, and any of the other major gland areas. I think this has to do with the ebb and flow of the tides.

♋ They have a very ticklish nervous system.

♋ Cancers are usually sweet-looking, with oval faces. You want to crawl into their laps and tell them all your problems. The Cancer is always very sympathetic, very maternal and nurturing.

LEO

L eo is the purple sign, the color and sign of
royalty. Their number is one, and in its sin-
gularity, it takes on the leadership quality. Leos
are usually perfecting the themes (see Sylvia's
book, *Soul's Perfection,* for a list of all 45 life
themes) of Activists, Cause Fighters, Manipulators, and Loners. They have a determination of
will that carries them far.

Leos have been given an unfair shot by
being told constantly that they're pompous.
Actually, they have a tremendous amount of
insecurity, which makes them bark loudly. I
feel that the Leo can be a very, very addictive

personality if badly afflicted. But I think that their insecurity drives them to this addiction, and also to overachieve.

Leos have a strong degree of fidelity—possibly the strongest in the zodiac. They become totally hurt and disemboweled by broken relationships, and they take guilt totally upon themselves because of any break in a close relationship.

Leos have a way of saying things with a very sarcastic flair, but they're totally honest and justice minded, as are Libras.

Leos are very health oriented; they never want to be nonfunctional. A lot of signs share this worry in their mind, but Leos will also worry about this in their body. They go along with the old idea: a healthy body, a healthy mind. At times, they can be very obsessive about health and nutrition, almost to the point of hypochondria. However, they're not continually obsessed with their health—only at certain times.

There is nothing sadder than disappointed Leos, unless it is hurt Cancers (who, as I told you, make you feel tremendously guilty when you emotionally injure them). But a Leo can become wrathful if someone they love is hurt—even a slight hurt. All of the fire signs are like this. They will turn to you and say, "What did you mean by that, when you said . . . ?!" They can say things to others, but God help you if you say it to them. If you ever get into a fight, you want a fire sign right beside you. You do not want any other sign, except maybe a Cancer.

Leos can spot flattery, but they can also accept constructive (and destructive) criticism; they simply evaluate what is said. Leos will barge right into a conversation because they're so afraid of forgetting something. And don't leave a Leo in the dark about anything! They don't like it at all. You will also find them being possessive about what they have, but not stingy.

Leos will usually be found dealing in the mind area, in psychology and the like, although they don't get into it in depth like a Sagittarius or Aries does. But the Aries should work with handicapped people, because they go over things so many times.

Leos are very intelligent, and this is not a slur, but they know a little bit about a lot of things. This makes them great conversationalists—they love parties. There is nothing more attentive than a Leo who feels you have something to say.

If Leos like you, they will put you on a pedestal. They are lovers of children and underdogs. They have a way of telling everyone else about the person they love, but they rarely direct these emotions to the loved one. They feel that it would make them more vulnerable. So when their loved one comes along and says, "I heard what you said about me," the Leo will say, "Yeah, you're okay." But when talking to a third party, they will eulogize you.

Leos usually marry for keeps, and they're very idealistic about marriage. If they marry more than once, they will carry the burden of the failure of the broken marriage for years.

Leos usually want to take their children everywhere with them. All fire signs are that way. If they are invited to a function, they always ask, "Can the kids come, too?"

Leos long for material gain, but often they

do not want to work too hard, or climb that ladder for it. Leos don't like jobs that get their hands dirty. They do not like abject poverty either. Although they work to help the world, they will not get knee deep in the dirty clean-up jobs in the ghetto. They would rather earn money from afar, and then send it to the poor.

Leos hate to lie, and usually they avoid it at all costs. God help you if you lie to a Leo. They take this as a personal affront. And this sets up a vicious circle, because then you tell more lies to the Leo so that you don't get into trouble for the first one.

Leos take pride in their accomplishments. They always want their companions and children to be well groomed, looking as nice as possible. They also want their homes to look nice, but paradoxically, they don't want to spend any money to get all of this done. Figure that one out if you can!

You cannot push bad merchandise off on Leos; they are too shrewd. Even when buying a car, they will not think a thing of asking the dealer to show them the original invoice.

Leos love the outdoors and all forms of

nature. Most Leos have green thumbs and work well outside. They can make anything grow. Leos also enjoy games. They really hate to lose, and sometimes to keep peace, it is advantageous to let the Leo win (or any fire sign, for that matter).

Leos are very patriotic: "Mother, John Wayne, and apple pie." You really never find a Leo being subversive. And they're not really bigoted, either—they don't approve of that type of thing at all.

Leos are very spiritual, even if not structured in religious norms.

Leos have a brilliant sense of humor, even if it does often border on the "Don Rickles" style. They can be so winning, though, that you find yourself laughing at yourself. Leos can also good-naturedly be the brunt of a joke. Leos have tempers, but usually it arises out of a deep hurt, rather than out of malice. They also tease unmercifully, but they stop if even one tear is shed. Leos are very moralistic, and rarely do you hear a Leo coming out with a graphic joke about sex. They will laugh, but they will not tell it themselves. They do not take well to the tacky or tawdry in life; it upsets them.

Leos have a strong tendency to question you at length, to provide reasons for your actions, or to explain why you said such-and-such. This is not being nosy as much as it is just an innate curiosity. Leos will take a big crisis very well, but it is the small, insignificant situation that other signs take in stride that will totally put a Leo off.

Nothing disturbs a Leo as much as having to deal with mechanical gadgets that do not work. They will start "do-it-yourself" projects, and will feel utterly defeated if it does not quite go right.

Leos will also obsess at length about why they're not better, and comparison factors with other people will rise up: "Look at so-and-so. She is the same age I am, and look how far she has gone." But this is not a martyred attitude like the Cancer would take on. (Although, as I said, Cancers have been badly discriminated against. We say they have a martyred attitude because they are so easily hurt; therefore, people think they are martyred. It is just that they are hurt all the way down to the bone. When you hurt a Cancer, it is bone deep.) Leos do not have a martyred attitude, but they do have a genuine concern about their position in life. They seem to look at other people as their progressive guideposts.

Leos' voices are magnificent, and they always sound as if they could sing beautifully. So when you get Leos on the phone, they will always have a resonant voice. You will never hear a Leo squeaking. Even the females have a very deep, resonant voice, or a very mellow one. The air signs are the squeakers.

Leos have a strong flair for the dramatic, not in the "Sarah Bernhardt" way, which is for the Pisces, but they have a flair for a correct entrance or a powerfully delivered oration on a certain subject. If you watch Leos, you will see that they pick a time that is just right.

Leos are also good debaters, and they love to weave a trap around the people they're doing battle with. They can, by most standards, be very rude, but you forgive them because there's no malicious intent. They will simply state, "Why should I speak to them when I don't like what they stand for?"

Leo males are not threatened by females, and conversely, female Leos are not threatened by males. And neither one really understands how anyone can be threatened by the opposite sex. That is why liberation movements baffle Leos. They already believe they are liberated, and rightly so.

Leos usually answer to their own instincts. They are highly psychic in the area of natural precognitive abilities, not so much about people, as about events. Now, of course, people are attached to events, but when they're psychically reading, they will see more events, rather than people, coming into life. But both sides can be developed.

Physical Characteristics

♌ Leos tend to have trouble with their backs; for some reason, their backs narrow at the lower spine. In other words, they have very thick upper vertebrae, and as you get down into the lumbar area, it can become very thin. This can put a great deal of stress on the lower back, and like many Libras, they will have a swayback.

♌ Leos are also very neurologically prone, especially if they don't let all of their energies out.

♌ Leos have an angular structure, but they're beautifully formed people.

♌ They have beautiful eyes, and you're pulled to look directly into them. That's why Leos would make good hypnotists, although they don't stare at you the way Pisceans do.

VIRGO

The Virgo, known as "the Virgin," is promis-cuous. Virgos are also known as "the whores of the zodiac." Whenever I say that to Virgos, they say, "Yeah, that's right!" Any other sign says, "Oh, no!"

Virgos are promiscuous, but they have a prudish exterior. They are very sexually orient-ed, but they have an immense ability to subli-mate this sexual energy. They can redirect it, thank God!

Virgos like to have everything in its place, everything organized. Meticulousness is a trait of theirs. I do not think they're as nitpicky as they might think, though. They're not nearly as bad as the Capricorn. But you always feel embarrassed around the Virgo, as if they're cleaning up around you and dusting you off. That's why they often have cracked hands—they're constantly washing.

Virgos are very good with people, but they have to be absolutely sure of what they're doing. They need to be "on top" of everything, but they do need prodding. And they'll cover their tracks well, in a positive way.

When upset, Virgos are the slow, smoldering type. When in repose, they look unhappy or pensive. That's why a Virgo gets very aggravated, because people are always asking them, "Are you mad?"

They are retentive in just about all areas, with a file-cabinet mind, especially when they have been hurt.

Virgos are obsessive about colors in the house. They want the colors to match or complement well. And they have an obsession about counting. It is a very strange obsession. If they start counting 1, 2, 3 . . ., many of them will want to go all the way up to 100.

Virgos feel that they must finish everything. If they start making a dress, they have to finish it that night. And it doesn't matter if the sewing machine aggravates everybody—they feel you ought to know that they must get it done. They're also note takers; they carry lists constantly.

A soft heart (which is paradoxical of this sign) is another mark of Virgos. They will let their children walk all over them—they have little baby footprints all over their body. But no one else walks over them. And be careful of what you say around a Virgo; they can get upset over some off-the-cuff remark. That's how sensitive they are. The Virgo will reply, "I know it's not your fault, but you hurt me anyway." So don't say unflattering things to a Virgo, such as "Your nose does not fit your face."

A Virgo is also multifaceted (like the Gemini), and this leads them to need many people around them. Both the male and the female Virgo can be faithful to two or three at one time. Yes, it's true! And you cannot tell Virgos that they don't love all three of those people, because they do with all their hearts! They love totally.

You will notice, for some strange reason, that Virgos seems to run in groups of three. It's almost like they need three people to give energy to, and to receive energy from.

Virgos walk with their heads first, and on the balls of their feet. They have very defined laughs—usually high-pitched and somewhat hysterical. And they cry easily when pleased or provoked. They have a tremendous vanity streak, which stems from insecurity. Make fun of them, and you have an enemy for life; compliment them, and you have a friend for life. You cannot just flatter them, but given an honest assessment, they will accept it.

They are very close-knit with their family, even more so than a Cancer. And if there is any kind of dissension in the family, the Virgo will handle it. Some would say let the Libra handle it, but they're too busy balancing everybody. A Libra will drive everybody crazy, saying, "I see *your* side, and I also see *your* side," whereas the Virgo will say, "You're wrong, she's right; that's the end of it!"

Virgos are loyal supporters, and are more apt to be in the internal workings of an organization, rather than being the front-runners. Virgos are like Cancers—when allegiance is pledged, it's for life. They're more apt to keep their "friends" within a group made up of members than to have many outside acquaintances. Virgos have been known to be called fair-weather friends, but that's not the case.

Usually the first half of the Virgo's life is very introverted, and then all of a sudden they become extroverts. You can see a Virgo one day, and in six months, you won't know this person. All of a sudden, this individual has decided to be completely outgoing. Virgos usually don't get going until around age 40. This is because they don't feel particularly wise until then, and they're very slow to develop their self-image.

Virgos are permissive parents, but they're not consistent. A child will get by with something one time, and the next time, the Virgo parent will not allow it. So they're inconsistent. Their nervous system is highly tuned, so they have a tendency, after a long period of patience with a kid, to let out a shrill, high-pitched scream. There can be a moth or some bug, and you'll hear the Virgo shriek! But they do have a tendency to allow their children to get by with things that other signs will simply not allow.

The Virgo has a temper, but it is not caustic. They just get angry. The Libra individual will usually hit more below the belt than the Virgo, because the Libra comes from an emotional standpoint, while the Virgo comes in intellectually. Air signs do a good job of getting angry; but boy, if you're ever hit really hard by a fire sign, then you know it. The air signs come from the emotional standpoint, whereas the earth signs come from a very practical one. But fire signs go right to the heart.

Virgos are good talkers, and they usually relate strongly to their past. They have a tendency to look backward. Virgos have a tendency to say what they think: "Oh, when I was fat like you . . . !" or "Is that your daughter?"—(and it is your sister). They also have a habit of constantly putting their foot in their mouth.

If you give a Virgo a compliment, their eyes

fill up as though they want to cry. You don't know if you've said something right or wrong. Anything romantic or sentimental sets them off. Also, negative and positive vibrations give them chills. Corny or bad or good—whatever—they are always getting the chills.

It is hard for a Virgo to get started on things, and change is not to their advantage. They love well-ordered things, especially trips and new clothes. They also love to travel, and they can be ready on a moment's notice if they want to go. The paradox is that although they love travel and beautiful things, they will not go out of their way to buy or arrange anything. It is better, they feel, if someone arranges it for them, rather than forging ahead themselves.

One thing about a Virgo, if they like their house a certain way, it stays that way. Five hundred years later, you can go back, and it is clean and neat, but the stereo is still sitting right in the same place. You can always tell a Virgo's place, because when you take a picture off the wall, there will be white paint underneath, with green walls around it. They will just paint around their pictures, because the picture looks good there, and they don't ever want to move it.

Virgos are private learners—they're not geared much for formal training. They love the mystical, and they're not natural-born skeptics, which does not fit with most earth signs. You don't tend to hear a Virgo say, "I don't believe . . ." Once they accept a truth, then it is it for life. You never have to hassle a Virgo with skepticism. Virgos are the nicest people I ever have in the reading room. They will say, "Yes, I understand." And that's it. They love things for how they're presented—so they don't complicate faith, or even parapsychology. They just accept it. And they have marvelous retentive memories.

I have never seen a Virgo yet who did not have an estrangement with their mother. They may fight to overcome it, but it is always there. Then they make an almost undying effort to form a partnership relationship with their mother. In doing so, they alienate their father. They do have a tremendous closeness with brothers and sisters—even closer than with their mother and father. So in that way, they're good because they do not build up a symbiotic relationship with their parents.

The male Virgo is much more ambitious than his female counterpart. Both are very selective about the people around them. Unfortunately, the male Virgo (more than the female Virgo) could be classified as a fair-weather friend. This is because he will like you only for what you can do for him.

Physical Characteristics

♍ Virgos usually have ticklish stomachs; they are prone to stomach upsets and over-acidity.

♍ Their bone structure tends toward being small and petite.

♍ Virgos are not hypochondriacs, and they only care that their body functions right. They are not ones to go to a doctor, unless the situation really becomes unbearable.

♍   Virgos are absolute maniacs about their hair and complexion. They are so fanatical about their hair that you want to shave them! They are not blessed to be born with perfectly endowed features.

LIBRA

L ibra is my sign (I was born on October 19), the sign of the scales, which stands for justice. It is also the cardinal air sign. Libras will want to weigh everything; they are truly "middle-of-the-road" individuals. This can drive others crazy. Libras will see both sides of an argument, which makes them very proficient and dominant in politics and diplomacy.

If you ever see two people fighting around a Libra, watch how this individual becomes a mediator. Those fighting will say, "Well, they meant this . . . they didn't mean that . . . !" Then the fire sign will say, "I did too mean it!" Then the Libra will say, "No, no, . . . now, you did not mean to. . . ." And they have the tactfulness to do this. However, Libras are somewhat flighty people and tend to jump from subject to subject—and then they wonder why others have not kept up with them.

Libras are very expressive. Like Geminis, they will always use their hands when they speak. And Libras will always be seen or heard in some way—especially when they're small children. So you do not ever say to a Libra child, "Children are to be seen and not heard."

As parents, Libras believe that their children should just grow up to be "nice, clean, and not bother us." Libra is truly the partnership sign. Very rarely will you find unmarried Libras. They marry early in life and will often have multiple marriages. It doesn't necessarily mean the marriages won't work; it just means that they'll have many of them.

To Libras, any type of commitment is a marriage. If you say, "Well, you were only living with that person," they will reply, "It is just like a marriage." They may be "living in sin," but they do not want to tell you that they are!

Libra is the one sign that either marries early in life, has multiple marriages, or they *never* marry—ever, ever, ever.

If you want to get ten jobs done, give them to a Libra. Now, I'm not saying that the jobs will necessarily be done right, but Libras are absolute workaholics, and they're night owls, too. This is probably due to their hyperactive nature.

Libras, like Virgos, should be called "the prostitutes of the zodiac," which means that they can give their love to so many that they can love everybody! And they have a better time loving people magnanimously than they do one-on-one. So they will love you as a humanitarian—all over! They are very tactile, and will always want to hug and kiss you. And to Libras, if they don't kiss you, they don't love you. They seem to be very sexual, but they are more sensual than sexual. Beauty will turn them on more than a roll in the hay.

As magnanimous as they are, the paradox to most people is that Libras are secretive. You don't always know what's going on in their heads. If they tell you something, you may say,

"You say you have told me everything, but I still feel that you're keeping something from me." They leave you feeling as if there's a part still not understood.

Libras are also lovers of beauty. They can become very enamored with beautiful furniture; and anything that is created in an artistic fashion, such as jewelry, beads, and so on. Male Libras (like Sagittarius males) find themselves fascinated with gadgets such as watches.

Be careful of what you say and do around Libras, because if they feel they've been faulted, you will not go unscathed. Libras will track you down. They are known for their terrible tempers, and they're very verbal about it—but they don't let it show that often. They will go after your vulnerable spot. The one thing about Libras is that if they take part in a fight, they want *you* to throw the first punch. If you don't, they can't fight you. So the worst thing you can do to a Libra is say, "Oh, I'm sorry," just when they're getting ready to let you have it. You just have to let them get it all out. Otherwise, when you do commit some insignificant infraction, the Libra will let you have it anyway!

Libras tend to "suffer in silence," but they hate martyrdom. The worst thing you can say to Libras is that they look down, or tired, or seem to feel under the weather. They're really concerned about being an imposition, which will drive everyone else crazy. Their friends will say, "Why don't you ever tell us *your* problems?!"

Don't try to give Libras advice about themselves—never do that! If they want help, they'll tell you. But by the time they tell you, it is usually too late to do anything for them—they might be dying by then! Their delicate balance negates advice because they're too busy externalizing to worry about what's going on internally.

Libras are very empathetic people, but they see illness or being maudlin as an act of weakness. They have a very high pain tolerance; if anybody could get an appendectomy done with just a local anesthetic, a Libra could.

Libras are not patient with interruption of ideas or business dealings. The reason for this is that they get sidetracked too easily. Their minds work very rapidly, and they have very busy minds. Therefore, any outside influence is usually spurned until Libras get what they have to say off their minds. One thing I've noticed about Libras is that if you say something to them, they will act like they're ignoring you. They'll turn their backs on you, then come back later and ask what you said.

Libras usually have the ability to cut through the fat in an argument or a comment and get right to the heart of the matter. If you compliment Libras, they appreciate it, but they really don't take it to heart, so it's lost on them. Apple polishing is not effective, because they don't know what to do with it. You can butter them up one side and down the other, but it doesn't faze them.

Loyalty is very important to Libras; they detest ingratitude. As a result, Libras are very hard taskmasters—not only for themselves, but for other people as well. They are not domineering bosses, but people always wonder how they're going to keep up with them. The Libra is blatantly honest—to a fault—like the Sagittarius individual. But you're never in doubt around them.

Libras are also "head" people, and they

love to pursue profound ideas—usually their own! They have a depth that even they don't understand, which helps no one, including themselves. They are the "baubles, bangles, and beads" sign, but underneath all of this can be found a very controlled mind. Sometimes they're *too* controlled, and they can be very stubborn. Libras, like Sagittarians, are really a "don't fence me in" sign. They don't like it, and they will not put up with it.

All Libras are more partial to their fathers than to their mothers. This is true even for the males. And Libra is the sign that definitely carries both masculine and feminine traits totally. They will alternate these sides back and forth within the hour! This can become very confusing.

One thing you'll never want to do around a Libra is act affected. If you suddenly start to develop a southern drawl, the Libra will say, "Why are you talking differently?" They do not like affectation in speech—not even in their own speech.

Physical Characteristics

♎ A true Libra is usually light-haired and has light eyes (blue, green, or hazel).

♎ As mentioned earlier, Libras tend to be hyperactive.

♎ They are very glandular people, and go to fat very easily.

♎ They also have a tendency to have problems with their hips. I know many, many Libras who have bad hipbones.

♎ Also, I don't care how petite Libras are—when they walk around, you think it's a 300-pound truck driver coming along. Personally, I've always been very enamored with the way people walk, since they say that body language tells a lot. I don't care how you sit, stand, lean, or whatever, but watch a person walk. That gives you every indication of what the person is like.

SCORPIO

Scorpio is the sign of regeneration and prop-
agation. Even though Scorpios are guided
by their genitals, they are actually directed
toward business goals. It is true that the
Scorpio has a criminal mind, but these individuals can turn it to their advantage and do well
in business. You will find that some of the
world's greatest leaders have been of this sign.

Scorpios are very vital to all forms of business, and they're quite goal oriented. Like
Virgos, they will sublimate their energy into
their goals. For example, you will never see a
Scorpio become a real estate agent and stay an

agent for long. The Scorpio will become a broker and have their own little company.

Scorpios do not like being in a subsidiary position, and they always have goals, goals, goals. They will have goals for the year, and say to others, "Out of my way!" However, they will not step on people to achieve their goal. They simply don't want you standing in the middle of their road when they are on a full roll.

Scorpios tend to be very secretive, more so than the Pisces. They're even secretive within themselves. They are the kind to whom you will say, "What is the big secret?!" And they have no clue what you're talking about. Whereas the Pisces will try to verbalize their thoughts, Scorpios don't even bother—they can't. And I think it has to do with their unbridled sexual energy. They really don't know why they are that way. (Unfortunately, a lot of winos and derelicts are Scorpios.)

Scorpios really want to change things—they want to change the world. Now, they don't want to change their homes; they won't bother with that. They want to change the PTA, their community, and God. I think God is a Scorpio.

You can suffer around Scorpios, and they won't have much empathy for you. Paradoxically, they may express sympathy if you have a hangnail, but they show no concern if you're cut from ear to ear. The Scorpio will ignore it and not even tell you that it will be all right. Now, if Libras are approached by someone with a hangnail, they say, "You don't know what suffering is! I'll tell you what suffering is!"

If you want to go to somebody that will really make you crazy, it's a Scorpio doctor, because if you walk in with a headache, the Scorpio doctor will say, "Gee, it might be a brain tumor!" They give you the worst shot first—always. And you say, "Why did you tell me that?!" They reply, "I want you to be prepared so you won't get upset." Too late, Doc, I'm already upset! Scorpios don't even think that their actions are malicious; they're simply preparing you.

Very rarely will you see Scorpio doctors in malpractice suits, because they've covered all their tracks. They do this in love affairs, too.

They check you out carefully to make certain that you have stamina. (They might even check your teeth to be certain you have overall good health.)

If there is any phobia a Scorpio carries, it is a natural fear of death or annihilation. Also, since Scorpios rarely get depressed, when you do see one who is, this person must be in a very, very bad state. Nothing is halfway with the Scorpio.

Scorpios really take charge of things. I have found, as with most signs, that the male is harder to handle than the female, unless he is rounded out by other traits. But the male Scorpio is harder for others to take, as he often comes across as arrogant and pompous. Also, he feels as pompous as he looks, unlike the Leo male. If you think the Leo has a regal bearing about him, the Scorpio comes in like, "Here I am!" and expects to be greeted with shouts of "Hurrah! Hurrah!"

Scorpios are very big on red, maroon, and magenta, even more so than Leos. They have rich, inflated tastes. The disconcerting thing about Scorpios is that it will take them forever to get up enough ardor to go into battle about anything. You say to them, "Are you going to get up and fight for this?" And they reply, "No, not right now. . . ."

Scorpios are very, very cheap—not with themselves, though. If they want to go to a movie, and there's no one to go with, they'll treat you—but only because *they* want to see it.

They also naturally horde things. Scorpios save springs, tin foil, spools, and all that kind of junk—because they never know when they might need it. And you should not ever dare to throw anything away that belongs to a Scorpio.

Both male and the female Scorpios can drive you crazy, because they're always looking for a verbal battle. They want to be the head of anything they can. If you want a committee started, give it to a Scorpio. They will chair the committee, arrange everything, and do it themselves.

Scorpios do not carry a lot of insecurity, like the other signs do. That is why other signs think the Scorpio is so pompous. They simply feel that when they are right, they are right, and that is all there is to it!

Neither the male nor the female Scorpio is interested in raising children. They enjoy *making* them, but they don't want to keep them!

Scorpios are the loners, the overseers; they are secretive and magnanimous. They must get the broad overview of the picture. And they're the ones who are 99 years old and still handling everything. You very rarely see a Scorpio become senile. Water signs have a tendency to get senile more easily if they don't watch it.

Scorpios are also fastidious cleaners. Now, the amazing thing about this is that they will clean the hallway, but not their own room. So the hall will be nice for someone walking down it, but their room might be a nightmare. Or they'll keep the windowsill clean, where no one will ever look. And they're the kind who will go around straightening pictures on the wall. They'll say, "Oh, wait! You have a loose thread hanging on you." They're always fiddling around you. "Here, let me fix your collar for you." It's a nice gesture, but after 20 minutes of it, you get fed up.

Don't ask a Scorpio to return any clothes. They will wear them, even if it chokes them to death. They will not take anything back and say it doesn't fit. If they wear a size-6 collar, and you buy them a size 5, they will wear it, choking, with their eyes bulging out. If they get rancid food, they will eat it, or leave it, but not return it.

Scorpios have a different moral code. I don't mean to say that they're rotten, but it would be nothing for a Scorpio to smuggle something if they thought it was needed. Other signs, however, would be too intimidated to do something like this.

Scorpios can lie to you with all truthfulness—do you know what I mean? They work out of their own set of truths, and they don't think it's wrong, because it's not wrong to *them*. You cannot say to a Scorpio, "That's wrong!" They will give you a perfect, idealized answer that is absolutely right. And I'm certain that the old adage, "Every man must find his own truth within himself," was written by a Scorpio.

Scorpios are tremendous teachers, and they love to be educated, so you'll find them going to school for 5,000 years. They also make great pharmacists and are often involved with medicine. In fact, if you tell Scorpios what medications you're taking, they'll go and look at the bottle. They might not know what it is, but they want to look at it anyway.

Years ago, Scorpios were very heavily into sorcery, alchemy, chemistry—anything that had to do with the natural forms of life. But strangely enough, they do not like bloodletting of any kind.

Scorpios have a natural stamina. You have to be careful with them because they're the sprinters in life. Scorpios will have three or four things going on at once. They'll have two full vocations going on side-by-side, without one just being an avocation, like the rest of the signs. For example, a Scorpio might be both a concert pianist and truck driver—totally different jobs, taking up maybe six to eight hours each.

Physical Characteristics

♏   Scorpios tend to have problems with the reproductive system.

♏   Like Pisceans, Scorpios usually have dark hair, but if they're not dark-haired, then they have very luminescent eyes.

♏   Scorpios have a lot of dimples.

♏   Scorpio women have a tendency to do lovely things with their hair—they have beautiful manes of it.

♏   Like the Libra, a Scorpio can put on weight very easily. But Libras usually battle with it most of their life, whereas Scorpios can put it on and take it right off.

♏   Scorpios get very barrel-chested, like opera singers.

SAGITTARIUS

NOVEMBER 22–DECEMBER 21

Sagittarius, the Archer, is a very analytical sign. Sagittarians make particularly good researchers, doctors, biologists, botanists, and psychiatrists. You will find a tremendous number of psychiatrists under this sign. Most of the time you will find a Sagittarius going into some kind of work in the area of the mind. Even if Sagittarians work as mechanics, they're still going to be very enamored with what happens within the mind of a person. So they're very prone to exploring others from a psychological perspective.

Sagittarians, male or female, have an

endearing quality whereby they constantly ask, "I'm all right, aren't I? I feel good, don't I? I'm having a good time, right?" They constantly need to be validated, yet they're not a borderline personality.

A lot of people will be thrown off by Sagittarians because they don't seem to have minds of their own. It turns out that they absolutely *do,* but they still want others to reinforce them. There again, that's what their whole mental process is like. You must constantly soothe Sagittarians. If there is any sign that is filled with anxiety, it seems to be this one. Unless they're completely quieted down by air and water signs in their chart, Sagittarians will be very anxiety-ridden people. And I think that's because they work so much from their intellect. They will usually migrate toward somebody who says, "Shhh, yeah, everything is just fine." Then they're fine, and they can go on and analyze and do their own number. But every once in a while, they have to touch home base.

Sagittarians are tremendously quick-witted. They not only enjoy a joke, but they can tell one very well. And they have a highly developed sense of humor. (Just as an aside, I think that people who do not like animals, children, music, or have no sense of humor are insane—I really do.)

Sagittarians write very well, but they're very wordy and a little bit boring. If you read anything by a Sagittarius individual, you may say, "Would you please get to the point?" They ramble on and on because they want to cover all bases. They even do this when speaking. (But they're not nearly as nitpicky as Capricorns, who want to tell you what suit they were wearing, on what day of the week, and how the weather was that day.) If you ask them to repeat one word out of a book, they will repeat the entire book instead. Or if you want to find out about a movie, they will tell you the entire plot.

A Sagittarius will explain and postulate on every side of a subject: "Now, if it happens this way . . ." "Now, if it happens that way . . ." "Now, in case it should turn around and go the other way . . ." So they have all of the bases covered. They don't want any loose ends.

Watch Sagittarians buy something. They can have a fit around anybody they're buying a car or house from. They will go through everything with a fine-tooth comb. "Well, what if the tires wear out? What if the carburetor doesn't work right?" And pretty soon you're ready to just give it to them. "Please, just take it off my hands, and get out of here!" It is usually very hard to drive a bargain with a Sagittarius, because you usually end up saying, "Just take it, I don't care." Often, Sagittarians will be the kind of people who would come to a class and say, "I'll pay you after I find out if I like it." This is typical behavior for them.

Sagittarius is also a "don't fence me in" sign, just as Libra is. Sagittarians are tremendous freedom lovers. And you never, ever want to make them feel like they have no freedom. Now, what is crazy about Sagittarians is that they'll stay in the house forever . . . until you tell them they must leave. And then, boy, you've had it! But they'll stay forever in one singular place.

As long as you do not put a time schedule on Sagittarians, they're fine. Now, what is unique about a Sagittarius is, if you happen to be a freedom-loving person involved with one, for some reason they become very possessive. If you turn around the other way and become possessive with a Sagittarius, this person will bolt on you. It's weird—you never know what to do with them, whether you should be free and outgoing with them, or be possessive. So you stand in front of Sagittarius individuals and ask them constantly, "What do you want from me?"

It is never boring to be with Sagittarians, and I think what makes it all worthwhile is that they are so witty and so marvelous to be around that people usually migrate to them. They always have a group of people congregating around them.

Most Sagittarians do not come into full bloom until later in life. Many of the signs are like this, in fact, but this is especially true of Sagittarians.

Sagittarius is also a very, very faithful sign. These individuals do not love three people at once the way Virgos do, but they can switch loves very quickly. And they can change allegiance totally, within a matter of a few weeks. They can be totally ingrained in one family, home, and everything; and then completely move their whole household somewhere else and begin with another spouse and a whole different family. They will be sublimely happy and feel like they've been there forever.

Sagittarians love children and are very concerned about them. And if anyone cries around Sagittarians, they will immediately melt. They will crumble. You don't want to cry around them because they'll get more upset than you are. They bark very ferociously, but drop one tear, and they usually say, "I didn't mean it." Then two hours later, they'll tell you what they thought about it. And when a stranger comes up crying, it upsets them terribly. It is a unique quality about them. They won't get as upset with somebody crying within their own family as they will with a stranger.

Sagittarians will do everything for someone else—clean their house, scrub their floors . . . while their own floors can go to pot. So they're truly magnanimous as far as helping people on the outside. And it truly is this sign about which others will say, "Well, why doesn't charity begin at home?" Sagittarians don't want you to talk about that.

Sagittarians, like Scorpios, can be quite vindictive. Most of the signs can be, but these two signs are spiteful to the extreme. They are the kind of people who will say to you, "I haven't spoken to my mother or sister for 20 years—and I don't care to." You'll ask them if they feel bad about this, and they'll say no. They'll say it to you in words like this: "They committed a mortal sin—they interfered in my life." So if anyone close to them really interferes, really judges them, they can erase them from their lives. And they don't seem to carry any guilt about it. That person no longer exists for Sagittarians. And no way can you try to make peace for them. If you try to have a little dinner and all of a sudden the sister shows up, the Sagittarian will walk out the door. They have no qualms about being rude on that score at all. There is no way of welding the situation together.

Sagittarians are very blunt. If you visit them at home too late, they'll say, "I'm sorry, I have to go to bed." Then they'll walk into the other room. These are the types of people about whom you might say, "They're truthful to a fault!" And then you go, "Oh!" when they put their truths in motion. But it's funny—these Sagittarians don't understand why people always seem to feel so wounded around them. Unfortunately, you'll have no room for a retort, because you know that what they've said is the truth. But you say, "Did you have to say it that way?!" And they'll reply, "If the truth hurts, too bad!" or, "Well, you ought to know it's true," and they'll watch you bleed. But they'll also try to bandage the hurt right away because they're so sorry about hurting you. Sagittarians mean nothing by it.

Full-blown Sagittarians can get away with saying things that others cannot. You can walk up to the exact same people and say the same thing that Sagittarians do, and they'll punch you right in the nose. Sagittarians say it with a smile on their face, and people say, "Okay." But another sign will try to go up and mimic a Sagittarius and get stabbed to death. People are so enamored by Sagittarians' charm, and their beautiful ways, that they don't really know that they've gotten it real good until maybe days later. People will say, "What the hell did they mean by that?"

It's not uncommon to walk up to a Sagittarius, be totally whittled down, and then say, "Thank you." When you walk away, you may think, *I was had!* Yeah, but it sounded so beautiful when they said it! A man who came to my office one day was a Sagittarius. He said, "I don't know what I expected, but you're not it!" I said, "Oh, thank you." About two days later, I thought about it and went, "Hmmm." That is what Sagittarians do—you can go four or five ways with whatever they say. You're constantly saying to Sagittarians, "What did you mean by that?!" And they think you ought to know.

Sagittarians have such a total intellectual approach to everything that they just assail you. Even their sex life is very intellectualized. This is also the sign that gets drunk on words. Sagittarians just overflow with words—beautiful ones! Everything sounds melodious, and it flows together very well.

Physical Characteristics

♐ Sagittarians usually have either reddish hair, or the complexion of a redhead.

♐ They are usually ruddy-complected people and have a full mane of hair. If they're male, even though they may be going bald, they will have big tufts of hair around the sides. It seems they have hair all over them—everywhere.

♐ Sagittarians tend to be either very far-sighted or nearsighted, and they almost always have an astigmatism.

♐ They tend to have problems in the lower back area. Most of the time they come into life with a curvature of the spine. They are very swaybacked.

♐ Sagittarians are usually tall people—very, long of limb, with short trunks. I take on the Sagittarian aspect—I have legs clear up to my armpits—all legs.

♐ They usually have very small hands—
regardless of their stature. Sagittarians
have very petite, dainty hands, and the
nail beds do not go very deep.

♐ Usually Sagittarians are large-structured
people. Even if they're slender, they still
have a large bone structure and are very
angular.

♐ They also have very, very luminescent,
shiny eyes. If you have ever seen Andy
Williams, I am certain that there's a
Sagittarius somewhere in his chart,
because his eyes always shine as if
they have drops in them.

CAPRICORN

DECEMBER 22–JANUARY 19

Capricorn is the strongest sign of the zodiac. Now, all of you can scream and argue about this, but it's absolutely true. This is the endurance sign. If you notice, in any group there's always a Capricorn acting as a leaning post, holding everybody together.

The Capricorn has a heavy intellectual side that almost always seeps into the emotional area. People say, "Gee, Capricorns are so intellectualized," but they're so much that way that they're almost frantic about it—I don't think people realize to what extent. It is intellectualized emotion, as opposed to the Sagittarius individual, who has the pure intellect. Even Virgos tend toward intellectualizing the metaphysical aspects of life.

Capricorns are the plodders; they love obstacles. Watch them—if there's no Mt. Everest, they'll make one just to prove that they can climb over it. If you don't give Capricorns a challenge, they become very irate and fidgety. Now, they're not trouble seekers, but they're definitely the planners, absolutely determined to succeed in any venture. "Here is something I plan to do, and by God, I'm going to do it!" They may even go out and tear up the whole backyard just so they can tell you how tired they are.

Capricorns are analytical to the point that it really drives you crazy. They will say, "On Tuesday, no it was Wednesday—because on Wednesday it rained, and I wore the blue suit . . . . no, it couldn't have been the blue suit, it was pin-striped. No, because that was the day I wore the . . ." By the time they get through, you don't really care what they're saying! Air signs will not be able to listen to such nitpicky details. They will just blow it off and forget it.

If you start nitpicking with air signs, they will go right up the wall, saying, "Cut that out!"

Capricorns, like Sagittarians, will not only tell you which movie they saw, but will compare it to all the other movies they've seen, citing the dialogue of each. They've memorized the dialogue, of course, and they will tell you that so-and-so sang this, then they will *sing* it for you! And then so-and-so looked at their horse and said such-and-such. They have all of the minute details. They will even tell you about the interior of the theater, how they got there, what they ate before . . . as if you give a darn, right?

One marvelous thing about Capricorns is their tremendous retentive memory. If you ever cause any kind of a stink with these individuals, they will name the date and the time that you caused it.

Capricorns are totally analytical about everything. They will also correct you on things you originally said. They will say, "Could I have that again, please?" When you repeat it, they may reply, "That is not what you said. You left out the 'if' from the second phrase. It is not *exactly* the way you said it the first time. You actually said it like this . . ." Yes, they've got terrible retentive memories—to the point of exasperation, and you say, "I don't give a hoot how I said it. Did you get the concept?" And with no obvious bother, they reply, "No, the concept is not right unless you get the wording right."

Capricorns are not the phobic ones of the zodiac. You very rarely see true Capricorns with a full-blown phobia. They don't tolerate it. You won't find them with a height fright (acrophobia) or fear of wide open spaces (agoraphobia) or whatever. They simply do not have any time for it.

Capricorns are great humanitarians. They will tell you that if the world was how they wanted it to be, everybody would be better off, because everything would be systematized. They're sweet and easy to get along with—they really are. They're not vindictive, and I think they have the most wonderful laugh in the world. You can never get too mad at them. They start out with a "ha-ha," and then they burst into this marvelous laugh (whereas Virgos laugh through their noses—snorting).

Capricorns love nothing more than poking fun at themselves. They are the best sports of the zodiac. You say to the Capricorn, "You walk like this . . ." and they will die laughing. Do an imitation of them, and they also erupt in peals of laughter. Everyone should have a Capricorn as a pet.

The Capricorn is really quite fenced in, very internalized. They do have depth—their retentive memory shows that—but they do not want people to know their vulnerable spots. That's why parents should be very careful with these children—Capricorns are among the most sensitive signs of the zodiac.

Capricorns do not have time to bleed over things; they are not a superficial sign. In fact, the air signs are more superficial than the earth signs, unless there is something else in their chart that is very strong. You'll find that most of your Libras, Geminis, and Aquarians are super-ficial in their behavior.

If you show Capricorns beyond a shadow of a doubt that your way is better, they will totally do it your way. And if you get them to believe in something, such as parapsychology, they are usually lifetime believers. They're like that about anything. If they believe in something, they believe in it for life. They continue to be into something long after everyone else is sick to death of it. They are not faddish people.

Capricorns are immaculate dressers. They have a beautiful way of knowing what colors go with what. Capricorns, even if they're casually dressed, will look like they did it on purpose. Nothing is askew with them. I know many Capricorn people, and when they dress sloppily, it is done on purpose. My brother-in-law is such a typical Capricorn that even when he is in his ricky-ticky-tavey clothes, he has little matching tennies, little matching shorts, and a little matching top. He says, "I really look like a slob," but of course he looks just fine.

Capricorns are tremendous spenders. Here is where they are a little faddish, which does not fit them at all because nothing else in their life is faddish. But if someone shows them a chrome bird that hangs and is a new thing, they'll buy it. If they go to an antique store, they'll buy the kewpie doll with the clock in its stomach, and put it up on the mantel. You say,

"Yuck!" But they do it almost for the shock factor. I think it's the only thing they do to shock you, but they really feel that the item is gorgeous. Of course, they will tell you, "If you don't want it, I do . . . I just love it!" And you say, "Oh, it's nice!" My brother-in-law has a rooster with metal stuff hanging off of it, which sits on his stereo. This thing is horrible, but he loves it.

If you go into a true Capricorn's house, you'll think you're in a hospital. Everything is clean and in its place. Capricorns can get upset over soap that's smeared on the side of the sink, so they have to have everything nice.

They also go in for very, very spicy foods. You will see Capricorns adding chili pepper and Tabasco to everything. Both males and females will neglect their bodies, then they'll suddenly go on a ferocious health kick. They tell you they're going to fast, jog, and eat sunflower seeds for three years. What's also marvelous about Capricorns is that they have a tremendous resiliency in health. They can break everything in their body, and two days later they're up running around, but they're also very paranoid about their health. If they're phobic about anything, it's their health. So you'll see them going for long bouts where they're into health food, jogging, lifting weights, or whatever strikes them.

The Capricorn is usually very well charted, except for a few paradoxes, such as buying those crazy things and a few health kicks. But usually, you can chart Capricorns right down the line because they follow a set pattern.

You will not usually find a Capricorn with an addictive personality. They simply won't stand for it. If they ever drank too much, or smoked pot in their early days, they will usually right themselves immediately. They will tell you they don't like it, and they never did like it, and they don't like anybody that does like it, even though they were into it at one time. They're not really affair people, speaking of sexual affairs. If they ever do happen to get into infidelity situations, they're usually very morose and penitent about it. So they're not the philanderers of the zodiac.

The sex life of Capricorns, like Sagittarians, is usually very intellectualized. Now, there is something everybody wants—an intellectual sex life! They intellectualize everything. Put hand here, rub three times, rotate, cut on dotted line—they're directing the entire time they're making love. However, they don't like crude language, swearing, or obscenity. Libra males, on the other hand, are the lovers of the zodiac. They say, "Come here, baby!"

Capricorns will start reading something and become obsessive about it. Not only that, but they're in love with words. They don't have a large vocabulary, but if you give them a word such as *sycophant*, they will say, "Oh, that's lovely . . . what does it mean?" Then they'll use the word in a sentence. They are the people who like a "word of the day," and the next time you hear them talk, they will have used your word. It is usually in the wrong place, but who cares?

Physical Characteristics

♑   Capricorns are prone to have neuralgia and arthritis. They really have a problem with their joints, which stiffen up, crack, and creak at a very early age. They snap, crackle, pop, and can actually sit there and crack their ankles and elbow joints to pieces. It's caused by dry sockets. They need an awful lot of oil and lubrication. They really ought to take lecithin, vitamins A and E, and lubricants because they're so creaky!

♑ Most of the time, any kind of arthritic problem is due to a person having too much unbridled energy. A Capricorn has such energy, and it goes into their joints. So tell Capricorns very early in life to dissipate some of the energy they carry. This will help prevent the arthritis from developing. But watch out—telling Capricorns to slow down for a while is like giving them a death sentence. They have to lie on the outside of the covers in a hospital, knowing that they can get up at any time. They don't like to be sick.

♑ If you notice, Capricorns have very small faces and heads. They are truly the pinheads of the zodiac. They are very well formed, but they have these little, itty-bitty faces. And you wonder, if you look at true Capricorns, how they get everything into that one little space—eyes, nose, mouth, and so on. They usually have very sharp, prominent features, which helps with the optical illusion of the small heads.

♑ Capricorns always look intellectual. Did you ever see a dumb-looking Capricorn? They always have a way of looking smart. You never see a Capricorn walking around looking like they're saying, "Duh."

♑ Even if Capricorns are tall, they always look somewhat delicate. They can be very tall, strong as a horse, and very angular looking; but they have a delicacy about them—even the males. You're afraid that they'll break, or that they're not too sturdy. They have small bones.

This is very deceptive, because they have tremendous stamina. So don't be thrown off by this delicate, dainty stuff.

♑ Capricorns are very finger- and hand-oriented people, too, which is quite unusual for an earth sign. You will see them moving their fingers or their hands a lot; rubbing a thumbnail, or rubbing or fiddling with a finger.

AQUARIUS

<hn>JANUARY 20–FEBRUARY 18

Aquarius is an air sign. Aquarians are natural born teachers, and they are also tremendously magnanimous. Like Libras, they can love many people collectively, yet they have a very hard time with one-on-one relationships. They are the ones who love humanity *en masse*.

Aquarians prefer to be with more than one person. They will say, "Let's go see so-and-so." They play much better to a crowd than one-on-one. You always want to say to Aquarians, "Aren't you happy with me?" They reply, "Oh, I'm happy with you, but let's go see Janice and

Bob anyway." They always want to talk to somebody else, and play to a larger group. For a while, they'll play to just one, but that gets very tiring for them because they're actually "on" so much of the time that it's like they're performing. They are the natural performers of the zodiac. Give them a spotlight, and they just go to town.

Aquarians are totally appealing. People will invite Aquarians to just stand around and perform for them. You'll always find Aquarians at a party with a group around them, holding court. And if you don't listen to them, they'll shout everyone down because their voices get higher and higher. Soon they're yelling, "Now, listen to me!" They're very polite, but you *are* going to listen!

Aquarians love to dance. And even though they're an air sign, they love the water. Take them to the ocean and they just quiet right down, which is possibly the only time they ever do. Aquarians are very difficult to figure out. They have a tremendous loyalty factor, but sometimes you don't know where it is, because they can switch their allegiance so fast to the other side (like Sagittarians).

People are often very confused by Aquarians and want to ask them, "Are you mad at me?" You never know exactly how they feel about certain things because they'll get a very stern face. A lot of times they're very preoccupied with something, and they don't mean to ignore you, but it makes you want to say to them, "Is it something I did?" They won't understand what you're talking about. They say, "Oh, no, it has nothing to do with you."

Aquarians are a paradox, as they can become introverted while they're extroverted. They'll seem to be very outgoing, but they also seem to have a hidden compartment. They almost make you internalize yourself for some reason. So people are constantly approaching an Aquarian and saying, "Are you okay? Are you mad at me?" The Aquarian will say, "Of course I'm not mad at you!" But you're never really quite convinced of it.

Even though Aquarians are very extroverted, you say, "What's hidden?" They're like the Pisces in that way. They assimilate an awful lot from the Pisces individual. Also, they can suddenly get mad at you for something you said two years ago, and it has finally dawned on them. They don't have the "file cabinet" mind of the Libra, but they can instantly get angry at you.

With Aquarians, anger builds up over a long period of time. You'll already be over whatever it was, yet they're going to tell you about it eight to ten months later. They're totally furious at you, and it's usually over some small thing. This leaves you to say, "Huh? Well, why didn't you get mad at me when I hit you over the head?" The Aquarius individual will say, "That wasn't what bothered me—you spilled a drop of water on me, and that was what did it. And you did it on purpose, I know you did," which is very confusing to the normal person.

This is a very complicated sign, very complicated. Anybody who has Aquarian friends or acquaintances will find them highly complex. They seem somewhat detached a lot of the time. I think that's what makes you say, "Where are you?" and makes a rational mind say, "What?!" They're so totally paradoxical. They can seem to be detached, and jump from subject to subject, yet they can get completely involved with something for a moment, a day, a year, and then they're done with it all. It's a washout for them. You'll say, "Don't you like . . . ?" and they say, "Well, I did, but I don't anymore." They can be totally engrossed in something and then bang, they're off and running on a whole new subject, leaving everybody else saying, "Huh? You were here, and now you're way ahead over there. . . ."

Aquarians cannot understand why you don't keep up with them. They really fly when they get going. It's very hard to buy them a present because they may be tremendously enamored with something one month, and then be into other things the next month.

Aquarians are also very romantic. They're tremendously in love with love. To make Aquarians cry, let them read *Wuthering Heights,* and they will get totally hysterical.

Aquarians are very ingenious. They are the kind of children who will hook up all kinds of marvelous little things from nothing. A spool on a pencil can be a microphone to them.

A comb on a box will be their typewriter. You can give them anything to play with. They're marvelous.

Aquarians are the ones who say, "Doesn't that remind you of such-and-such?" It could be a little hole-in-the-wall, and they'll say, "Doesn't that remind you of a tunnel?" They have a natural naïveté that is very endearing. And you really can play a joke on them. Even if they walk through the same door twice and an object falls on their head, they will walk through it again. They have a very definite childlike quality. They can be 70, and they're still childlike; and I don't mean senile. It makes everybody want to give an Aquarian some- thing, because they'll go on and on . . . "Oh, it's just what I wanted, and I love it!" And they mean it.

Everyone should have an Aquarian as a pet. You want to pet them and love them. They're very endearing. They have a tremen- dous love of animals and hate injustice (like Libras); they can't stand it. They are the ones who would go out and march for the seals or the whales or whatever. They just can't tolerate anything that is hurt, maimed, or downtrodden.

Aquarians will also write letters about things they don't like. They are tremendous letter writers, and they'll want to know why you didn't write one, too. If they don't actually write the letter, they'll write it in their mind. Tell an Aquarius individual that something unjust has happened to you, and this person will be the first sign of the zodiac to say, "Oh! That's the most horrible thing I've ever heard of." They are very empathetic, so Aquarians are the best people to go and relate any injustice to, because they'll get just as upset as you are about it.

Aquarian males are far more fluky than the females. You really don't know where they're at. The female Aquarian usually has a lot of stability, but the Aquarian male is "constant to one thing—never," as the saying goes.

Most Aquarians like the outdoors, but the conditions must be nice. In other words, they *will* go camping, but they better have the best during the trip. They don't want all that dust floating up all over them, getting them all dirty and grubby—no way! They're the first ones to go wash their hands and say, "Okay, where are the showers?"

Physical Characteristics

≈ Aquarians are very sturdy and quite compact. Their bone structure is closely knitted together.

≈ They are usually of dark complexion— unless, of course, they have a very powerful Ascendant.

≈ When you hear Aquarians walk, you know they're coming. They have a very pronounced gait. I don't care how light it may be, they have a very definite, methodical step.

≈ When Aquarians stand, they do so with their knees locked, feet planted firmly on the floor. You can't budge Aquarians; you can't even knock them over. They make very good football players, as they don't fall down. Their stance is usually feet apart and knees locked.

≈ Both females and males have very broad shoulders.

≈ They are very expressive with their hands, as are all air signs, including Geminis and Libras.

≈ Aquarians are truly fidgety. They've always got something going—their hands, feet, arms, eyes—they just can't stay perfectly still—no way!

PISCES

The most striking thing about a Pisces—and you'll be able to tell it every time you see one—is that their eyes actually look luminescent. They are deep-set and usually dark, or are of a dark hue. In other words, if they have blue eyes, they are dark blue. There is no wishy-washy look about the eyes of a Pisces. Usually, the eyes are almond-shaped. They have the most marvelous eyes, with a natural contour of the eyebrows and lashes. Everything from the nose on up is absolutely phenomenal. You look into a Piscean's eyes and you really think that you've seen eternity. Any color is gorgeous and almost luminescent.

Pisceans have a disconcerting way of staring at you while you talk. You keep looking at them for approval, and they'll just stare. Now, they're really absorbing everything you say, but they seem to just stare at you. I think what happened was that somebody told the Pisceans when they were little, itty-bitty kids that having shifty eyes was a sign of weakness. So now they bore a hole right through you. Of course, if you tell a Pisces, "You're making me fidgety," they're very sorry about that, but they'll still bore right into you. And they have those gorgeous, luminescent eyes, so you're convinced that they see your soul anyway.

I have many girlfriends who are Pisceans. One was very typical; I would talk to her, and she wouldn't talk back. If you pause, then they'll talk, but they'll never break into your conversation and run over you with words, whereas air signs are always jumping in.

Pisces has, unfortunately, been given the slant of being the occult sign, which almost sounds hidden and subversive, but it's not true at all. They're not occult; they *are* metaphysical.

In fact, they're called the metaphysical sign. They are usually very spiritual people. Pisceans, by no means, like subversiveness in the sense of being occult. They would rather put it all out on the table. Then if it seems okay, they may absorb it, assimilate it, and file it.

Pisceans, both male and female, really love to be complimented—not flattered, but complimented. They will work endlessly for a compliment. In other words, if they paint a wall, they want to be told it looks nice, whereas the Capricorn couldn't care less if anyone notices how nice it is, saying, "I did it, and it looks good to me." The Pisces individual says, "Hey, look at that!" Their impetus is to work for a compliment. It is a tragedy when people are not complimentary around Pisceans, because they thrive on it. They want that applause and those accolades. You see, they're really saying, "Please, do you notice that I'm competent?"

Pisceans are deeply affected by any slights or insults and are really crushed by them. The other signs living around a Pisces say, "You've got to be kidding me! Did you really take offense at *that?*" But, oh yes, it does hurt the

Pisces. One good thing about Pisceans is that they'll tell you when they're hurt, whereas Cancers will not—they're the "suffer in silence" people.

Pisceans are also very intellectual as far as sexual relations are concerned. They love all the courting. They don't want it to stop—ever. Bring them flowers and bring them candy. Show them you appreciate them. Consequently, both male and female Pisceans make very good mates because they're so romantic. And it's not a false romance, because even after 15 years of marriage, they'll say, "I will put on my best clothes, and we'll sit down to a candlelight dinner." It's very nice. Even if they have intestinal flu, they want to sit down to a romantic dinner.

Pisceans are also lovers of beautiful things, like the air signs. They love things with beautiful form, such as birds and swans; and they love things with symmetrical, flowing lines. You can always spot a Pisces in a store, since they want to feel the texture of everything. You can never say to Pisceans, "If you touch it, you buy it," because they touch everything they see. They are very tactile and will compliment you, saying things such as, "That material is very lovely."

Pisceans are very aware of their bodies. You will always see Pisceans with natural agility. They are streamlined and svelte. They wear clothes very nicely, both male and female. They are the kind you can put into K-Mart clothes, and they look all dressed up. I think it's their natural bone structure. A lot of models are Pisceans, with high cheekbones. You never see a Piscean with a droopy, sagging jaw. They always have a very clean-cut jawline. In fact, there is an almost angular look to the jaw area.

Pisceans are the artists' models. They age very well, too. The only thing that a Piscean has to worry about is that, due to their bone structure and the cut of their jaw, they can get a little bit taut-looking when they get older. Because their jawline is so cut-in, they have a tendency to get a rigidity about them. However, very rarely do you see a Piscean needing a facelift, male or female. They keep that natural structure of the jaw. I will take the tautness over the sagginess any day.

As strange as it may seem, you won't find a lot of Pisceans in parapsychology. Now, that's strange because Pisces is a mystical sign. Yet, unless they're highly evolved, they won't be into parapsychology. This is due to the Piscean's very analytical, researching mind. Metaphysics doesn't give them enough solidity, so they negate it. If you *do* manage to get them into parapsychology, though, you'll truly have them. They'll say, "It sounds okay, and I'll dabble in this for a while," but they'll then run the whole gamut of the subject. They'll want to know the entire scope. They will try yoga, herbalism, astrology, and anything that they can actually put their hands on. Most Pisceans, once they've been bitten by the parapsychology bug, will usually go all the way. They'll be dedicated to it for a whole lifetime, since they don't switch allegiance very fast.

Pisceans are tremendous readers—they'll read everything—cereal boxes, food labels, and so on—but they don't get into groups easily. They almost have to push themselves to get out into groups. This usually starts at about the age of 25, an age when they really have to force themselves out. They'll have a wealth of knowledge, but they're private students, rather than group studiers. Pisceans are avid learners and note takers. They take notes on everything and don't want to miss a word. Walk into a class, see a Pisces, and say, "Hello, there." They write, "Hello, there." You'll say, "Nice day," and they write down, "Nice day." If they miss a word, they'll turn to the next person and ask what the whole sentence was. They don't want to miss anything. They'll tape-record a lecture and take notes, just in case the tape fails. If you tell them something, they'll write it down, and they'll quote you.

Pisceans are a paradox in a way. If you want to tell them a secret, they'll keep it forever and ever and ever. They figure that if you were strong enough to give them the secret, then they should be strong enough to keep it. They're not rumor mongers, and they're the first ones of the zodiac to say, "Cut that out; he's not here to defend himself!" Now, Capricorns *do* have a tendency to swap stories, but not on a malicious level. They're only doing it for information. Aquarians will dabble in rumors, but don't keep a secret from Pisceans—they'll become very hurt if you do, because you should know automatically that they have a great deal of integrity. They would never tell a soul.

Pisceans are very stubborn. They have a tendency (like all of the air signs) to feel that if they're right, they are right all the way down to the bone marrow. And boy, you'd better not shake them up. Pisceans are good debaters, too. When they know that they're right, they usually have the information to back up their stance. If that doesn't work, then they'll hit you in a sensitive area. "Well, if you do that, it will hurt so-and-so." Then, of course, you're totally disintegrated. Pisces are called the "goody-two-shoes" sign. They will say, "You didn't mean to hurt them anyway, did you?" And you say, "No."

Pisceans, like Capricorns, will change their minds if you prove to them that they're wrong. Whereas, to change the mind of an air sign, most of the time you would have to kill them. And the Taurus, if you show them that the moon *does* come up, they'll deny it—no way, it does not, no . . . and that is the end of that. They say, "I know what I know, and it is finished, over, and don't talk to me about it anymore."

And finally, you will never find a Pisces acting like a bigot. This sign despises prejudice and bigotry, which is certainly a good thing these days.

Physical Characteristics

)(Pisceans have very beautiful, luminescent eyes, and their eyebrows and lashes are finely contoured.

)(They have high cheekbones and a clean-cut jawline.

)(With age, they do not sag, but they may become taut-looking.

About the Author

*Millions of people have witnessed **Sylvia Browne's** incredible psychic powers on TV shows such as **Montel, Larry King Live, Entertainment Tonight**, and **Unsolved Mysteries;** and she has been profiled in **Cosmopolitan, People** magazine, and other national media. Her on-target psychic readings have helped police solve crimes, and she astounds audiences wherever she appears. Sylvia is the author of **Adventures of a Psychic; The Other Side and Back; God, Creation, and Tools for Life;** and **Life on the Other Side,** among other books.*

Please contact Sylvia at:

Sylvia Browne Corp.
35 Dillon Ave.
Campbell, CA 95008
(408) 379-7070
www.sylvia.org

Hay House Titles of Related Interest

BENEATH A VEDIC SKY: A Beginner's Guide
to the Astrology of Ancient India,
by William R. Levacy

BORN TO BE TOGETHER: Love Relationships,
Astrology, and the Soul,
by Terry Lamb

COLORS & NUMBERS: Your Personal Guide
to Positive Vibrations in
Daily Life, by Louise L. Hay

HEALING WITH THE ANGELS
ORACLE CARDS,
by Doreen Virtue, Ph.D.

✻ ✻ ✻

Tune in to **HayHouseRadio.com**® for the best in
inspirational talk radio featuring top Hay House
authors! And, sign up via the Hay House USA Website
to receive the Hay House online newsletter and stay
informed about what's going on with your favorite
authors. You'll receive bimonthly announcements
about: Discounts and Offers, Special Events, Product
Highlights, Free Excerpts, Giveaways, and more!
www.hayhouse.com®

✻ ✻ ✻

We hope you enjoyed this Hay House book. If you would like to receive a free catalog featuring additional Hay House books and products, or if you would like information about the Hay Foundation, please contact:

Hay House, Inc.
P.O. Box 5100
Carlsbad, CA 92018-5100

(760) 431-7695 or **(800) 654-5126**
(760) 431-6948 (fax) or **(800) 650-5115 (fax)**
www.hayhouse.com®

Published and distributed in Australia by:
Hay House Australia Pty. Ltd., 18/36 Ralph St., Alexandria NSW 2015
•*Phone:* 612-9669-4299 • *Fax:* 612-9669-4144 • www.hayhouse.com.au

Published and distributed in the United Kingdom by:
Hay House UK, Ltd., 292B Kensal Rd., London W10 5BE
Phone: 44-20-8962-1230 • *Fax:* 44-20-8962-1239 • www.hayhouse.co.uk

Published and distributed in the Republic of South Africa by:
Hay House SA (Pty), Ltd., P.O. Box 990, Witkoppen 2068
Phone/Fax: 27-11-467-8904 • orders@psdprom.co.za • www.hayhouse.co.za

Published in India by: Hay House Publishers India,
Muskaan Complex, Plot No. 3, B-2, Vasant Kunj, New Delhi 110 070
Phone: 91-11-4176-1620 • *Fax:* 91-11-4176-1630 • www.hayhouse.co.in

Distributed in Canada by:
Raincoast, 9050 Shaughnessy St., Vancouver, B.C. V6P 6E5
Phone: (604) 323-7100 • *Fax:* (604) 323-2600 • www.raincoast.com

❋   ❋   ❋

THIS IS THE NEWSLETTER YOU'VE BEEN WAITING FOR . . .

Order your subscription today to the *Sylvia Browne Newsletter*, and receive an exclusive lecture CD from psychic Sylvia Browne—absolutely FREE!

Right now you have the chance to hear from your favorite author and psychic Sylvia Browne—six times a year—in the pages of this remarkable new newsletter!

As a subscriber to the newsletter, you'll learn inside information directly from Sylvia Browne. You'll find out how to connect with your angels, learn about the Other Side, and get Sylvia's latest predictions as well as information on how to get and stay healthy.

You'll be the first to hear about the latest psychic discoveries of Sylvia or her psychic son, Chris Dufresne. Also, your subscription allows you to write to Sylvia—and one of your questions may be featured in an upcoming newsletter along with Sylvia's answer.

Exclusive Sylvia Browne Lecture CD—FREE!
With one-year subscription to *The Sylvia Browne Newsletter*

Call **800-654-5126** to order your Subscription and FREE lecture CD today!

www.hayhouse.com®